Adrienne Brady was born in Burma and grew up in Surrey. Marriage and four children took care of her creative energies for a good number of years. An honours degree in English and History and a master's degree in creative writing acted as a springboard for writing her own poetry and to satisfy a deep-rooted ambition for travel and travel writing. Since 1987 she has lived overseas in Singapore, Brunei, Libya and the Middle East taking opportunities to explore ancient and lost worlds as well as to capture them in words and on camera.

Based in Dubai from 1996–2006, her travel features were published regularly in Gulf newspapers and magazines. From a home base in Devon and more recently Dorset, she has continued to travel as well as completing three memoirs: life and travels in Libya under sanctions, travels throughout Oman and into Central Africa and a trilogy of adventures into Asia, the Gulf and Europe. *On the Trail of Saint Paul* focuses on a series of journeys made to those places that are a legacy to Saint Paul on his first and third missionary journeys and his final journey to Rome, as well as places that are a legacy to those who were influenced by his Word, primarily the Order of the Knights of Saint John and the Crusaders.

Adrienne Brady is also a prize-winning poet. She lives in Dorset.

Also by Adrienne Brady

Non-fiction
Kiss The Hand You Cannot Sever
Melrose books

Way South of Wahiba Sands – Travels with Wadiman
Austin Macauley Publishers

Danger Zones and Pleasure Zones
Austin Macauley Publishers

Poetry Anthology contributions
Quintet – Staple, UK

From Then till Now
Poetry Press U.S.A.

Basic English Series, Poetry 2
Go and Open the Door, Poetry 3
Macmillan Education, UK and Australia

Let me be me …. a junior anthology of poetry
Macmillan, Swaziland

Summer Comes Barefoot Now
Editor – EPB, Singapore

Magazine contributions include
The Spectator, Poetry Review, Wexas Traveller

Success as an international prize-winning poet led to an entry in
The International Who's Who in Poetry and Poets' Encyclopaedia

For my friend and travel companion, Jill Good.

Adrienne Brady

ON THE TRAIL OF SAINT PAUL

Adrienne Brady

AUSTIN MACAULEY PUBLISHERS™

LONDON * CAMBRIDGE * NEW YORK * SHARJAH

A CIP catalogue record for this title is available from the British Library.

ISBN 9781398465756 (Paperback)
ISBN 9781398465763 (ePub e-book)

www.austinmacauley.com

First Published 2023
Austin Macauley Publishers Ltd®
1 Canada Square
Canary Wharf
London
E14 5AA

As always it is the people, I travel with who make my expeditions possible. Heartfelt thanks to Father Paul (Maddison) for arranging such a diverse and truly amazing pilgrimage to Palestine, Father Mark from Saint Mary's RC parish, Poole for inspirational, spiritual leadership; Declan (Rev), Eunice and others for behind-the-scenes work; fellow pilgrims from St Mary's RC Parish for welcoming me, a stranger in their midst, to share an unforgettable journey.

This is also in memory of my late partner and travel companion, Richard Chapman, who lost his life to cancer shortly after our journey through Cyprus. Special thanks to my friend, Jill Good, who accompanied me on expeditions with RSD Travel Ltd. through Turkish occupied Northern Cyprus, two expeditions through Turkey – guided tours through Ephesus, Rhodes and Crete as well as two visits to Malta. Further thanks to the guides and drivers from RSD travel Ltd for safe journeys through the troubled land of Turkey. Finally, once again thanks to Father Mark and fellow pilgrims from Saint Mary's – especially Lorna and David Watts for their friendship and editing comments on the pilgrimage to Rome and Assisi which bring *On the Trail of Saint Paul,* to a close.

Map of Paul's Third Missionary Journey, thanks to Jasmine Brady.
Illustrations, thanks to Beatrice Gray
Photograph selections and jacket cover photograph
copyright Adrienne Brady

Photographs of the Acropolis and View to Saint Paul's Bay, Lindos, Rhodes, thanks to Jill Good

Thanks to Editorial Consultant, Rodger Witt

Thanks to Oliver Jefferson and the editorial, production and promotion team from Austin Macauley for their work in bringing *On the Trail of Saint Paul* to fruition.

Transcription of place names: to reserve the wide divergence of place names in the countries visited – spellings vary considerably in books and on maps – I have endeavoured to select the most straightforward.

Cyprus: first published in *Way South of Wahiba Sands* by Austin Macauley in 2013.

I wish to acknowledge the following from which I have quoted.
George Mc Donald, *Cyprus Spiral Guide* (AA Publishing 2006)
William Dalrymple*, From the Holy Mountain* (Harper Perrenial, 1997)
Davd Suchet, *In the Steps of Saint Paul* (BBC Documentary)
Juliet Rix, Malta and Gozo (*Bradt Travel Guide, Edition 3*)

I have drawn upon a wide variety of sources during my travels. Opinions and errors are mine. I am especially indebted to those authors mentioned in the Bibliography. Every effort has been made to contact the copyright holders of quoted material. Late responses and inadvertent omissions will be rectified in further editions.

Table of Contents

Foreword

Such was my interest in the success of missionary work of the disciple Paul, as well as its impact on civilisation that despite the ongoing dangers that travellers face to this day in Palestine, Turkey and even Malta I decided to take opportunities when they arose to visit those places that are a legacy to his missions. My journey starts in Jerusalem the shrine of three faiths – Christianity, Judaism and Islam – the most fought after city in the world. All three faiths share origins and beliefs in Jerusalem as the centre of Divinity – the prime place on earth where God meets man. It is also the place, along with Damascus where the newly converted disciple Paul started his mission to spread the Word of his new-found faith. Such was the life-threatening hostility he faced from his preaching both in Damascus and Jerusalem that he had no option other than to flee for the safety of his home in Tarsus to give himself time to recover and prepare for what lay ahead.

Although to this day Paul continues to be a controversial figure – admired by some and vilified by others one cannot but be impressed by the astonishing determination of this man who, despite the life-threatening dangers he faced was prepared to travel by boat, on foot or by donkey to establish the Christian faith throughout the northern shores of the Mediterranean. Furthermore, in addition to preaching on his travels, he also wrote a series of epistles that provide an insight into the beliefs and controversies of early Christianity – predating the Gospels and Acts of the Apostles, they are believed to be the oldest texts published in the New Testament. At one time all thirteen of these epistles were attributed to Saint Paul – over the years, while seven are accepted as being entirely authentic and dictated by Saint Paul, the authorship of the others is believed to have come from more contemporary followers writing in his name. Nevertheless, he is one of the most prolific contributors to the New Testament. Unlike the followers of Jesus in Jerusalem Paul decided not to follow Judaic law. This appealed to the gentiles and gave it global reach thereby creating Christianity as we know it today.

*****

A pilgrimage to the Holy Land with fellow parishioners from Saint Mary's Parish, Poole was a stepping stone for the first leg of a journey *On the Trail of Saint Paul,* and those disciples whose determination to spread their Christian belief took them on evangelising missions into and through the length and breadth of the ancient world. From the Holy Land my travels continue to those places in the region of the Mediterranean visited by Paul on his missionary journeys as well as on his journey via Malta to Rome. Malta is next on the agenda. After two years imprisonment in Palestine Paul is sent via Malta to Rome to stand trial before Caesar for preaching Christianity.

Finally, a visit to the magnificent basilicas dedicated to Saint Paul and Saint Peter, the first Pope in the beating heart of Rome: the Eternal City and official residence of the present Pope. I then head into the Umbrian Mountains to Assisi – the former home of the Saint Francis, whose life of humility and service to the poor so influenced the current Pope that he chose to be named after him.

Palestine Pilgrimage

'Thou art Peter, and upon this rock I will build my church and the gates of hell shall not prevail against it and to thee I will give the keys of the Kingdom of Heaven'. (Matthew 16–18)

The Sea of Galilee

Imagine the shore of the Sea of Galilee where a group of pilgrims gather on stone tiered seating. Before them, beneath a leafy canopy of sycamore fig a small round table serves as an altar where Father Mark is celebrating the first mass of our Palestine trip. As the pilgrims respond to the magical notes of Irena's flute, our voices soar over the lake where two fishermen are casting nets beaded with pebbles; swallows dip and rise over our heads – we are held in the deep embrace of the natural and spiritual worlds that surround us.

Here on the lakeside, a striking statue of Christ, hand raised over the crouching form of Peter, marks the place where He appeared to his disciples after the resurrection; nearby the Franciscan chapel: *Mensa Christi* – the Table of Christ – encompasses the rock that served as their breakfast table: powerful reminders that we are standing in the very footsteps of the risen Lord. The day culminates with a boat-ride across the lake. Surrounded by mist-clad waters, with wheeling, crying gulls circling overhead Declan reads the Apostle Mark's account of the calming of the storm uniting us once again in spellbound silence.

The downside to an organised tour that I feared: The crowds, the herding, plus unexpected low temperatures and the reality of coming face to face with armed Israelis guarding the encroaching wall, as well as inspecting our coach were to come. They were a stern reminder of the continued threat of violence and displacement suffered by the Palestinians we shared mass within Beit Sahour. Nevertheless, these encounters were more than surpassed by the engaging people we met and amazing places we visited.

Among them the crowd-packed scene in the Church of the Holy Sepulchre: Byzantines, Crusaders, Armenians, Eastern Orthodox and Latin Christians have served to keep this church the most visited place in the Holy Land. On our journey along the *Via Dolorosa* – Way of Sorrow – we take turns to help carry a full-size cross through the narrow, crowd packed streets of Jerusalem's Old City, Father Mark leading the way and the prayers. While some shopkeepers and passers-by ignored us, some stopped to stare while others joined us in prayer – a reminder of the agonising past.

Inside the church, the dark cathedral-like space is over-filled with people and over-cluttered with décor: a congestion of chandeliers, decorative lights, icons and frescoes commemorate the final stages of the agony and death of Christ. As we join a shuffling line of pilgrims, while waiting for our turn to visit the tomb, the sense of spirituality begins to wane then, as if on cue, to one side a handsome Armenian priest – in colourful head gear and robes – takes centre stage to pray with his following of monks clad in sober black. Meanwhile, a line of Franciscan, candle-bearing monks are making their way towards a chapel, alongside the main building. Unable to resist the impulse to capture them on film I ease the long black lens of my camera between the shoulders of two leather coated male onlookers. They spin round. Anxiety is replaced by smiles when they see, not the gun they had feared but my camera.

As the emotive notes of the monks' Gregorian chant rises and echoes over our heads we begin to move forward and row by row descend worn steps to the Basilica of the Crusaders, built over the sepulchre. In the moment of prayer, as we take turns to place a hand on the marble slab that covers the tomb, a tangible sense of suffering and sadness takes hold.

*****

Each and every day of our pilgrimage begins by celebrating mass with Father Mark, in churches very often built by Franciscan monks on Byzantine and Crusader foundations commemorating a saintly person and event. Among those designed by the Italian architect Antonio Barluzzi – outstanding for innovation and simplicity of style – is the Basilica of the Transfiguration, marking the place on Mount Tabor where Jesus was transfigured in the eyes of Peter, James and John.

At 1850 feet, from two massive towers linked by a Byzantine-style arch, the basilica commands outstanding views across the hillside to fertile plains, Nazareth and the Sea of Galilee below. While inside, the dome of the apse features traditional Renaissance-style frescos of the transfiguration, the *piece de resistance* is the sky-blue dome over the altar where pairs of elegant, trimly attired angels with neatly cropped hair, guard saintly figures. The image of one pair – hands uplifted, eyes rolled towards heaven as if in disbelief, on either side of the transfigured form of Christ – holds a special place in my heart.

Mount Tabor, Mount Zion, the Mount of Beatitudes, the Mount of Temptation – each bearing an indelible stamp linked to gospel events and visited as part of our pilgrimage – none could compare with the Mount of Olives. It was here that King David fled from Absalom; Ezekiel viewed the heavenly chariots; Zechariah prophesied the End of Days, and it was from this very mount, where Jesus taught his disciples, that He finally made his ascent into heaven.

On this occasion we celebrated mass in the Antonio Barluzzi designed Franciscan chapel *Dominus Flevit* – The Lord Wept: fashioned in the shape of a tear, the exterior design of this small and extraordinary church symbolises the tears shed by Christ when He foresaw the destruction of Jerusalem. Inside

Byzantine floor mosaics and Crusader pillars add to a sense of connection with the past; while through an arch-shaped picture window – positioned directly behind the altar – an incredible tableau of the city of Old Jerusalem and the Mosque of Omar's glittering, golden dome unfold. A scene that enables us to imagine the sadness Jesus felt when He envisaged the destruction of the city He loved on his last fateful journey over 2,000 years ago: the Holy Temple towering over the Kidron valleys' palaces and white marble towers – its marble columns and great bronze doors shimmering in morning sun.

Our visit to *Dominus Flevit* prepared us for an on-foot descent, retracing the steps of Jesus to the Garden of Gethsemane; the Basilica of the Agony – built over the traditional Rock of Agony – the place of Christ's suffering, prior to betrayal and arrest – sports a lovely Bargello mosaic of Christ offering up both his and the world's sufferings on the outer façade. Ancient olive trees – the deeply gnarled trunks reaching several feet in width – add authenticity to the belief that they are the very same trees that stood in the garden at the time of Christ. A friendly interchange with an elderly Franciscan monk, tending the garden as his forbears have done over the centuries, contributed to the growing sense of the living past.

*****

On the final day of our journey through the 'The Holy Land', following moving visits to *Yad Vashem* – the Holocaust Museum on the road to Emmaus and the incredible Crusader Church at Abu Gosh – with original Crusader mosaics still covering the walls; we celebrated mass at *Ain Karem*, the birthplace of John the Baptist. At the start of the final, emotive hymn: 'Christ be our light', I became aware of a stranger in the row behind me. Tears were streaming down her face. My instinct was to move to her side and hold both my arms towards her. Her immediate response was to entwine her arms around my waist and rest her head on my shoulder. And so, we remained – comforter and comforted – in a tight embrace throughout the entire hymn: an unexpected and moving end to the Palestine Pilgrimage.

Ain Karem was also the staging post for the next stage of the journey to visit those places in the region of the Mediterranean that are a legacy to the missionary work of Paul and the disciples. Cyprus was on the horizon.

Paul's Third Missionary Journey

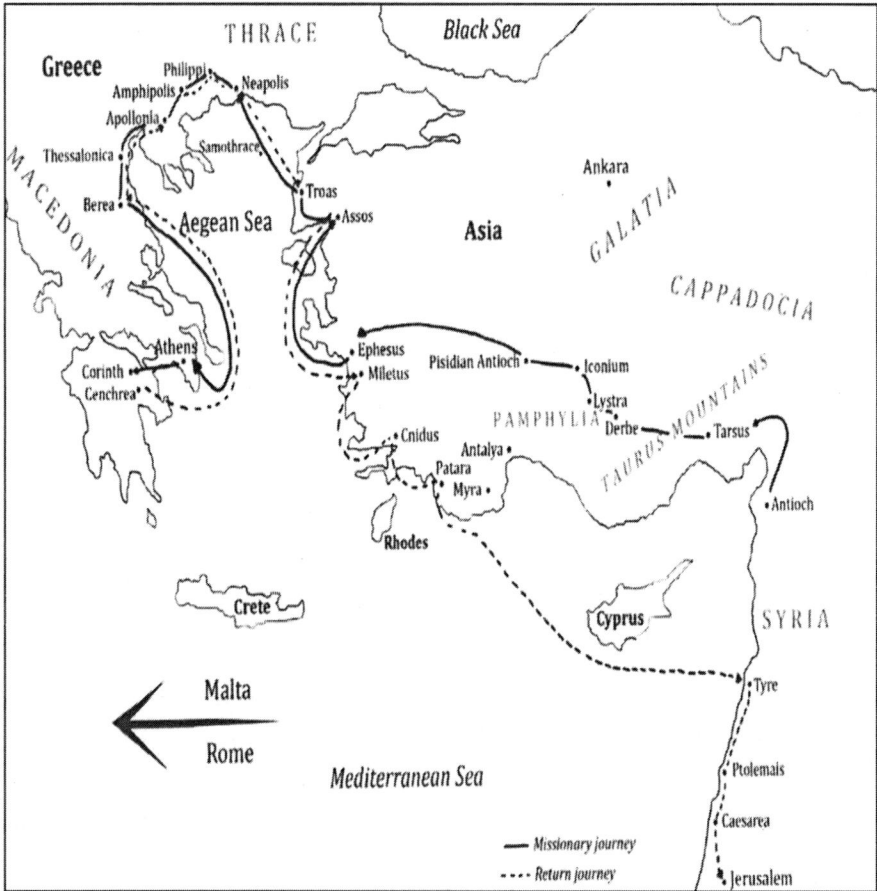

Cyprus

Island of Love

In A.D. 45/46 Paul, accompanied by the disciples Barnabas and young John Mark, a nephew of Barnabas set off on a cargo ship from Seleucia, Antioch's port in the eastern Mediterranean for Cyprus. (Acts 13). Barnabas, a native of Cyprus was used to travelling from his homeland to Jerusalem and Antioch but for John Mark, a native of Jerusalem, this was unknown territory.

In addition to visiting Pafos and ancient sites closely associated with Saint Paul the plan was to include the remains of ancient Greco-Roman sites dedicated to deities before the advent of Christianity. As well as Cyprus being a convenient stopping off place for the disciples, over the years many nations were drawn its shores: Phoenicians, Persians, Hellenes and Romans; Byzantines and Venetians; Egyptians, Ottomans and British to the Greek Cypriots and finally Turkish invaders, that occupy the north of this divided island to the present day. Between the 11th and 12th centuries the island was used as a retreat for those Christians attempting to defend their faith in the Holy Land: the Crusaders, the Knights Hospitallers and the Knights Templar.

Roman Ruins and Crusader Castles

Accompanied by my partner and travel companion Richard Chapman we set off on a visit to Southern Cyprus. Our travels were to be of the self-indulgent kind. Based at the comfortable Bay View Hotel, we were within easy reach of Pafos, the adjoining coastal region with its treasure-trove of ancient remains, as well as having access to the Troodos Mountains, home to the island's Orthodox monastic present and past. In spite of repeated attempts by Islamic forces to destroy it, Christianity in Cyprus showed a remarkable resilience and flowers to this very day. In the eight days at our disposal, our plan was to dip into the island's deserted and living past as well as to take the opportunity to meet up with expatriate friends who have made Cyprus a holiday retreat.

The following morning, Giorgios, our driver-come-guide was ready and waiting alongside his 4-wheel drive to take us on our mission.

"People swim to rock to find love," Giorgios explained as he pulled over at a cliff-side viewing point and pointed to the largest of a tumble of rocks, washed by luminescent waves: the celebrated Rock of Aphrodite, marking the birthplace of the Goddess of Love who, according to Greek mythology, was born of sea foam and drifted to Cyprus on a shell. To this day Cyprus is still promoted as Aphrodite's Island – 'the island of love'. Paul's message too was about love but divine love of a different order. An alternative name, *Petra tou Romiou* – Rock of Romios – refers to the Byzantine hero who hurled gigantic boulders into the sea to keep invading Arabs at bay. Both legends help to immortalise the mythical and historical past of the former Hellenistic and then Roman provincial capital of Pafos. It was from 1300 BC that the first waves of Achaean Greek merchants and settlers reached the island, spreading the Greek language, religion and customs. The cities of Kition, Kourion, Pafos and Salamis were established, and the cult of Aphrodite born.

Next on the agenda were the not to be missed 'Tombs of the Kings'. We followed Giorgios down carved, worn steps to the Egyptian inspired rock-cut tombs. Explosions of poppies invade courtyards where imposing columns and entablatures uphold the land overhead and guard the entrance to the ancient tombs. Raided but not destroyed the awe-inspiring City of the Dead was bathed in silence, broken only by the contented notes of nesting doves.

It was after the death of Alexander the Great that Cyprus came under the control of the Hellenistic Ptolemies of Egypt. Arches, pillars, ancient tombs and stone mosaics remain as compelling reminders of former lives and beliefs. There were no longer kings in Cyprus at this time – the 3rd century BC – but the internment of leading citizens of Pafos is reflected in their impressive atriums. Surrounded by Doric columns, burial niches have been cut and hollowed into rock walls. The sense of a hallowed place, where souls of the dead have been set free, endures. Now beyond the silence, the relentless grind of encroaching sea can be heard as it undercuts the cliff face, threatening to invade these once venerated chambers of a lost world.

We follow the coast road to the towering columns of Apollo's Temple; wedged against blue sky they create an imposing end to Kourion's Sacred Way. Herodotus wrote that, Greek colonists from Argos founded Kourion, the most impressive of Cyprus' sites. When the Romans took control, they adopted the Greek gods: Aphrodite became Venus, while Apollo Hylates: Protector of the Forests, took over from the Greek deity Apollo of the Woods. Fine Doric columns rise into achingly blue sky outlining the sanctuary and frame a walkway leading to a shrine, where the god was worshipped. An early convert to Christianity, the city suffered from Nero's persecution of Christians and suffered again from severe earthquakes. Kourion was rebuilt and then abandoned after devastating seventh century Arab raids.

The Odeon, a second century Greek then Roman theatre, takes centre stage. Built into the side of a hill overlooking the sea, its lovely location shows off to advantage curved stone seating that once accommodated 3,500 spectators. Far better suited to Greek drama than the savagery of gladiatorial Rome, the rejuvenated theatre has revived its classical beginnings: concerts and plays, staged throughout summer include performances of work by Greek dramatists and Shakespeare. That the Odeon's romantic setting also attracts newlyweds was clear. As we prepare to leave, one wedding party disappears, and another arrives: bride, groom and attendants distribute themselves among tiers of seats in preparation for a photo shoot.

Behind the theatre we follow a line of columns and partially rebuilt walls that outline the House of Eustolios: one of a number of excavated houses and villas belonging to wealthy Romans – each a depository for remarkable mosaic displays. After the earthquake of A.D. 365, Eustolios generously donated his baths and an annex of his house to the city declaring it to be a 'cool refuge, sheltered from winds'. A further inscription, referring to the 'venerated signs of Christ' that protect the house, makes sense when, from a raised wooden walkway, we look down on delicate pink and blue fish and bird motifs: Christian symbols, carefully preserved in mosaic floors.

Further uphill we skirt the remains of a 5th century Christian basilica, a Roman Forum and so much more that I was transported to time spent wandering through the remains of Libya's magnificent Roman coastal settlements. They too suffered a similar demise from earthquakes, marauding hordes and despotic invaders. Another surprise and reminder of my visit to Libya was a face-to-face meeting with the naked bronze form of the second century Roman Emperor,

Septimius Severus – last encountered in a more dignified pose at the entrance to the city of Leptis Magna, the place of his birth. This larger-than-life figure of the Emperor competes for attention with the sculptured marble statue of Aphrodite in the local museum. Immortalised as the ideal of feminine beauty in Botticelli's Birth of Venus, even without her arms, the graceful figure of the naked goddess continues to draw the crowds.

A truncated column, a saint and a legend: we were standing before a broken column. Named St Paul's Pillar, the column is said to be the place where the evangelist was tied and scourged for preaching Christianity. Today it was the focus of a bevy of cameras. On a more positive note, such was the success of Paul's mission that he converted the island's pro-consul *Sergius Paulus,* making Cyprus the first country to have a Christian ruler. (Acts 13) It was from this time that it is said that Saul changed his name to Paul. The tradition of Paul's scourging imbued the area with religious significance resulting in several churches being built on and close to the site.

A heavenward thrusting dome, seven colonnaded aisles, the swish of robes over mosaic floors, the fragrance of incense – I conjure the former glory of the fourth century Roman basilica of *Chrysopolitissa* – Our Lady of the Golden City. Thought to have been the seat of the Bishop of Pafos until destroyed by Arab invaders, the basilica was replaced in 1500 by the church of Agia Kyriaki – dedicated to Saint Kyriaki who was martyred under the Emperor Diocletian. Currently on loan from the Orthodox diocese, both Anglican and Catholic communities use the church – confirmation that, despite differences that arise in dogma and ritual, a shared core of faith remains at the heart.

Success on this island did not come without suffering. Appointed Bishop of Salamis, the place of his birth, Barnabas is reported to have been stoned to death by the city's Jewish community in (A.D. 61) and then buried secretly by his cousin, Mark the Evangelist, on the outskirts of the city. Four hundred years later Bishop Anthemius of Constantia (Salamis) found what was believed to be the place where Barnabas was buried – in today's Turkish north of Cyprus.

Recalling the mere outline of events so closely linked with the heart and survival of Christianity on the very soil where the Evangelists once stood was an inspiring end to a first day among the ruins. It also fuelled our interest and excitement for further discoveries and encounters in the days that lay ahead.

*****

The honey-coloured, stone walls and turreted battlements of Kolossi Castle glow in morning sunlight. An impressive reminder of the defenders of the Christian faith, this romantic medieval citadel became a stronghold for Crusaders when they were driven from the Holy Land. In 1191, Richard the Lionheart, leader of the Third Crusade, took possession of Cyprus from the Byzantine Emperor Isaac Comnenos, married Berengaria of Navarre and had her crowned Queen of England. A year later he sold the island to the Knights Templar. When the Templars were indicted for heresy, it was handed over to the deposed king of Jerusalem, the French nobleman Guy de Lusignan. The Frankish Hospitaller Kingdom, the knight founded, ruled Cyprus for the next three hundred years. Byzantine castles were refurbished, and cathedrals built.

As always, it is the artwork associated with those who lived and loved and died that keep the essence of what they were and believed alive. Beneath a mural of a cross on the east wall, I focus my camera on a coat-of-arms – Louis de Magnac's (Grand Master of the Knights Hospitaller) – then, on a carved block of stone, placed against the battlement wall I capture the Lionheart's Crusader shield.

Meanwhile, my Lionheart has moved on to investigate a ruined fourteenth century sugar mill. I find him inspecting an abandoned giant-sized stone waterwheel that once turned in the millrace of a nearby aqueduct. We are surrounded by overgrown land that replaced fields of sugar cane, wheat, cotton and grapes, once cultivated by the Hospitallers' servants on feudal holdings.

Like Kourion, the ancient city kingdom of Amathus enjoys a lovely coastal setting and complex history. While Richard has been distracted by a circling bird of prey, I focus on a line of marble columns – the remains of a colonnaded portico that once surrounded the white stone floor of the Agora complex – currently under restoration. Less upstanding outlines of the Acropolis, an early Christian basilica and baths unfold. The remains of circular stone houses and further extensive ruins of this once vast city cover the hillside and stretch to the coastline, where the Phoenician harbour and sections of the city walls have been lost to invading sea.

"It was the Arabs," a young attendant assures us as we prepare to leave the site.

"Arabs destroyed it."

History declares that Amathus was once an important Phoenician stronghold that sided with the Persians against the Greeks thereby retaining its eastern links via the gods worshipped here – Egyptian and Eastern, as well as Greek. An administrative capital in Byzantine times, it was also the birthplace of St John, the Almoner – the founder of the Order of the Knights Hospitaller. By 1191, when Richard the Lionheart arrived, Amathus was in decline. Ancient tombs were plundered and stones from beautiful edifices were taken to be used at the Crusaders' headquarters at Limassol. Then in 1869, the deserted city was plundered again. Dressed stone from the site was transported to be used in the building of the Suez Canal. Today, the Amathus Beach Hotel overlooks the sea as the city kingdom once did. Ancient tombs uncovered during preparations for the construction of the hotel continue to make for an uneasy alliance between past and present.

Brightly painted fishing boats and modern yachts crowd Kato Pafos harbour. The past emerged in the solid outline of the Ottoman fortress that overlooks the shoreline, while a line of half-submerged stones mark the breakwater that once sheltered Greek and Roman ships. Today, the atmosphere of this former busy trading port is relaxed; pavements overflow with street taverns and waterfront terraces. The place is so laid back that for locals and ex-pat residents alike, drinking and driving go hand in hand. John, an expat friend and recent offender, recalls the warning he received when he was stopped and tested by police: Found to be 'over the limit' – he was reprimanded by a wagging finger and a reprieve,

"Take care, you don't do it again!"

We sip glasses of Commandaria wine. Thick and sweet, not unlike a liqueur and produced from grapes grown in the Troodos foothills, it takes its name from the Knights' Commandery at Kolossi Castle. Highly regarded since Roman times, the vines cultivated by the knights were so esteemed that the King of Navarre transported some – Count of Champagne – on his way back from the Crusade: a reminder that even French champagne can lay claim to Cypriot origins. For Portuguese traders, shoots of Commandaria transplanted to their homeland produced a wine that was to become the ancestor of Madeira.

On a fleeting visit to the nearby House of Dionysus, we encounter the wine god himself; amidst sensuous mosaic displays he is in triumphal procession, riding a chariot drawn by two leopards. From a snaking walkway we gaze upon scenes of hunting, wine making and illicit love: Ganymede carried off by Zeus in the form of an eagle, Neptune falling for Amymone, and Apollo swooning for the love of Daphne.

As a second day among the ruins comes to an end, we make our way to the hotel. I plan to swim but just the touch of the pool's ice-cold water on one temperature-testing limb is enough to change my mind. I join Richard for a more relaxing option: sundowners on our balcony, overlooking the palm-fringed shoreline. We scan a horizon that has witnessed so many arrivals and departures; imagine Cyprus as a stepping-stone to the Holy Land, Antioch, Constantinople and Rome; examine maps for trails to tiny Byzantine churches, tucked into mountain folds; monasteries crowning valley heads. Across the empty bay darkening sea merges with the great dome of sky, releasing a shower of stars.

Of Monks and Monasteries

Stopped in our tracks by an angel hovering over the entrance to a cave, we pause to admire magnificent eagle wings and silken robes. In this delightful fresco, the solemn faced Angel of the Annunciation lifts his right hand over us with an air of poise and calm. A stairway takes us to an arched veranda that supports and provides access to the cave entrance.

This once remote spot in the Troodos Hills is where the twelfth century Cypriot hermit Neophytos sought a solitary existence. A small natural cave in a cliff face was the starting point. This he proceeded to transform into his *Engleistra* – enclosure – and then, by hand, hacked a small adjoining cell to serve as his bed, office and finally, his tomb. Ordained a priest in 1170 by the Bishop of Pafos, Neophytos' saintly reputation spread; the number of monks wanting to join him and the number of visitors wanting to meet him increased. To retain his solitude, the determined monk dug further cells above the *Engleistra,* one with an adjoining overhead tunnel. Intent on keeping his seclusion, he installed a ladder that he diligently hauled up after him.

On the outer walls, fading frescoes lose their heads and taper into obscurity. Inside, it is a different story. We come face to face with a line of forbidding monks. Forward facing in the Byzantine linear style, their soul-searching gaze penetrates the very depths of the soul. Holding crosses and parchments, inscribed with the formulae for salvation, their sombre demeanour casts a cloud of misgiving. Further into the cave, the outlines of more elegant saintly forms take on the curves and hollows of undulating walls. This fluidity of form gives these saints a more suggestive air of salvation. Even so, scenes of supplication and terrible suffering shroud the place in solemnity. The Nativity too is denied any sense of joy. Pious figures, painted in sombre blues and browns, stand in rows; soulful eyes stare into eternity.

The monk's cell with its rock-hewn tomb bears witness to the austerity of his life, and the fervour of his belief. Then an intriguing fresco of the saint, held between two angels, emerges. Hands crossed over his chest, the sombre Neophytos has grown wings and is at prayer, supported by the angels. The angels have furrowed brows and don't look too pleased with the charge in their grasp. Once again, solemnity overpowers any sense of joy.

A need to escape from a growing feeling of despondency takes me towards a shaft of sunlight slanting through the half open door. I breathe sun-flecked air and look down on the mellow stonewalls of the working monastery, the rose-scented garden and vine-covered slopes. Here, a sense of life and peace endures. Founded by the saint's followers in 1220, the seventeenth century restored church and working monastery of Agios Neophytos stand against the hillside, overlooking the hermit's caves.

Sadly, a series of unseen dramatic events were to bring misery not only to Neophytos and his followers but also to the Orthodox clergy and people. Seven years of tyranny from the self-declared ruler of Cyprus, Isaac Komnenos, were followed by the Crusader occupation. Cut from Byzantium, the Orthodox Church lost its authority and much of its property and sought the seclusion of the Troodos hills. A prolific writer, the saint expressed his anger towards invading Crusaders:

'Concerning the Misfortunes of the land of Cyprus…'

'England is a country beyond Romania in the north, out of which a cloud of English with their sovereign…sailed towards Jerusalem…But the English king, the wretch, landed in Cyprus. The wicked wretch achieved nought against his fellow wretch Saladin but achieved this only, that he sold our country to the Latins'.

Ancient Worlds LLC

Finally in 1570, tragedy in the form of conquering Ottoman Turks arrived. While the Catholic Church faced annihilation – on the plains below churches were destroyed, glorious Gothic cathedrals turned into mosques – Orthodox monasteries, including Neophytos were looted and sold, the monks forced to scatter. Ottoman cruelty and punitive taxation served to strengthen a quiet renaissance that had grown between Cypriot Orthodox, Catholic Christians and Muslims.

Then for Agios Neophytos, what seemed an end was merely sleep. Like the attacked and looted monasteries of Ethiopia, the monastery was reborn. In 1611, the monk Leontios began the work of restoration. Before us, the Venetian-styled dome of the basilica rises above honey-coloured walls. In spite of so much looting and destruction, Agios Neophytos monastery, church and museum, remain a treasure house of wall paintings, precious icons, sacred vessels and manuscripts, including the writings of the saint, attracting pilgrims and visitors worldwide.

Of Saints and Sinners

'When the church door opens and your eyes slowly adjust to the gloom, magnificent Byzantine religious frescoes begin to emerge, like photographs coming to life in a dark room'

George McDonald, *Cyprus/ Spiral Guide*

In the twelfth century, in the secluded wilds of the Troodos Mountains, a blossoming of Orthodox monasteries and tiny churches took place. Resembling stone barns, they remained unrecognised; unrecognised they remained unsought and survived as safe repositories of the nation's spiritual belief. This was the world we sought. A world of deep-rooted Christianity, vineyards and wineries – the ultimate survivors of despotic invaders – among the forested peaks surrounding modern Pafos.

Leaving the tourist zone of sunbaked beaches, banks and bars, hotels and restaurants, we follow an artery interweaving between red roofed villas, huddles of ancient stone houses, clutters of shops and roadside tavernas that stagger through banana plantations up vine-covered slopes to hidden churches and red-roofed, sky-reaching monasteries crowning valley heads.

The peaks of Troodos rise to 6,400 feet at Mount Olympus. Named after the Greek mountain home of the Olympian gods, its highest peak *Khionistra* (snow tipped) – marked by the white geodesic dome of a British military radar installation – appears and disappears as we climb and wend our way round tree covered spines that spread bony white fingers towards the plains below. Forming the island's mountainous backbone, the hills are snow-covered from January to

March offering skiing, and in high summer a cool retreat from overheated coastal plains.

High on the slopes, north of the sulphur spring resort of Moutoullas, we sought and found the eleventh century monastery of *Agios Ioannis Lampadistis* – St John of Lampadou; beneath a complex of pitched rooftops, two small Orthodox churches and a Latin chapel huddle side by side.

From the moment we step inside, what was plain and unadorned on the outside takes on a wondrous form. As our eyes adjust to the gloom, magnificent wall paintings emerge: faded coats of arms, lions and dragons of the Crusader world, and a Latin chapel where naturalistic murals and the Venetian love of colour combine. Saints with fluid outlines inhabit a geometric world showing a movement between Byzantium and Renaissance. Lithesome horses carry Magi dressed in flowing robes, to a Babylon that was set in stony desert alongside the Euphrates River. Further gospel scenes merge people, action and landscape in a world where beliefs and art styles meet and yet remain juxtaposed.

We stand and gaze in silent wonder, attempting to absorb the detail of Christ's triumphal entry into Jerusalem that grows from a nearby wall. 'No flashlights' the rules declare, leaving itching fingers and cameras that would flash of their own choosing impotent. Shutters closed.

In an adjacent isolated valley, we find *Agios Nikolaos tis Stegis* – Saint Nicholas of the Roof. We stand for a while taking in the remote hillside setting and stone-built walls that did indeed resemble those of a well-kept barn. The eleventh century cruciform church and monastery merits its title by the addition of a second overhanging tiled roof, affording extra protection against frost and snow to the original cross-in-square vaults with a central dome.

That the church and its treasure trove of frescoes suffered under the Turks is confirmed by the Russian monk and traveller, Basil Barsky. On a visit in 1735, he noted that it was a small monastery with two gristmills, many fields, and a forest enabling it to make enough money to cover Turkish taxation. There were no monks when Basil Barsky was here, but he was so enamoured with the place that he spent four days sketching the monastery and absorbing the beauty of the surroundings.

Today, the monastery attracts a constant stream of visitors. Each summer it becomes the spiritual centre of the lives of Christian groups who camp in the grounds. Its survival is said to be a miracle. In 1987, a fire spread through the camp, reaching the church walls. Just when hope was lost, the wind direction changed, blowing great tongues of flame away and towards the forest. The building was spared. Eyewitnesses believe that Saint Nicholas himself intervened preventing the fire from destroying the church and the extraordinary artwork within.

Inside, we pause beneath the crown of the dome. From over our heads the merciful eyes of Christ *Pantocrator* (Ruler of all) look down and into our very souls. In fact, the entire hierarchy of paradise appear: glorious angels, saints and sinners hands uplifted towards the heavens, as if the entire scene is about to unfold before us and the angelic troop burst into a magnificent 'Gloria in excelsis Deo'. More serious figures with deep staring Byzantine eyes emerge: Christ the alms giver; the handsome battle-clad haloed saints of Theodoros and Georgios, stand their ground, poised for action.

None can compare with the unique rendering of the fourteenth century Nativity scene of the Virgin mother breastfeeding the Divine child. A sense of naturalism and emotion flow from the womb-like globe encompassing the heavenly pair, who are surrounded by an angelic host, a shepherd playing a bagpipe, the Magi and earth-based souls that look this way and that as if communicating, one with the other, over the miracle that has occurred.

Said to be the loveliest of Cypriot churches, *Panagia Tou Asinou* – Our Lady of the Pastures – stands on a hillock in the shade of eucalyptus trees. From the outside, the utter simplicity of pale stonewalls against pine-draped hills takes the breath away. We fumble with cameras and then proceed to the doorway where again, we are stopped in our tracks. This time it is a fresco over the church door, which shows the founder kneeling and presenting his miniature basilica to Christ.

"I Nicephorus Magistro, a pitiful supplicant, erected this church with longing, in return for which I pray that I may find thee my patron on the terrible day of Judgement."

If we were impressed by the outside, then it was the inside that was overwhelming and, at times, confusing. Heavenly scenes slowly appear to reveal paradise that is at once available and yet held tantalisingly out of reach. I focus on the half-dome of the apse where Our Lady of the Pastures, flanked by two archangels, remains poised between heaven and earth. Crowding the wall, apostles and evangelists wait in anticipation. A sense of hope increases over the sanctuary, where the ascending Christ appears both majestic and stern while all about him his followers surge; their status symbolised by books or swords, they represent a strict hierarchy and dogmatic tradition in the world below. Furrowed brows and lifted hands are stern reminders of the need for penance.

Angels dressed in flowing robes hover between heaven and earth, over saints who reflect the triumph of heaven. Their straightforward gaze invites us to glimpse the spirituality within their souls. A throng of Orthodox saints we do not recognise gather about the one we do: Saint George sits astride his white horse with the boy who serves the coffee he demands before slaying the dragon, perched behind him – an idiosyncratic touch to remind us of his humanity.

If the hope sought by the onlooker is to be found, then it is from the dome of the narthex. Here, the kindly Almighty stares down from a star-filled sky; his unblinking and forgiving gaze offers salvation, while his thumb and third finger touch in the sign of an eastern blessing. Beneath him, a gathering of magnificent angels with powerful wings and golden ringleted hair unroll the heavens: an invitation we aspire to be worthy to achieve.

If there is a lesson to be learnt from the Troodos churches, it comes from the immediacy of the extraordinary artwork displayed on cloistered walls: a compelling visual representation of the church, conceived as a microcosm of the universe. From Christ *Pantocrator*, looking down from the star-filled heavenly dome to angelic hosts hovering over ascending saints, to gospel narratives and scriptures linking God to man in the world below.

The following day, our journey will take us to higher ground, into the realm of legends, heavenly glows and the outward show of glory.

Miraculous Icons and Stairways to Heaven

Dramatically sited high in the Troodos Hills, Our Lady of Kykkos – Cyprus's wealthiest and most powerful monastery – encompasses all the majesty of two thousand years of Christian heritage. That the monastery survived fire and the terrible looting exacted by the Turks in 1821 is something of a miracle. After executing the island's Archbishop and remaining bishops, Ottoman invaders are said to have carried away sixteen camel loads of gold, silver and objects made with precious stones. There is little of historical importance left except the monastery's most precious object – the icon of Our Lady of Mercy – one of several on this island, said to have been painted by Saint Luke.

While the Byzantine churches remained hidden and therefore safe, splendid Greek Orthodox churches and monasteries, like Kykkos, that announce their imposing and dramatic presence on hilltops and at valley heads suffered looting and attempts at annihilation, only to be reborn. The claim that supernatural power, rooted in icons of the Virgin Mary, is responsible for the birth and revival of at least three of the most magnificent of the Troodos monasteries continues to capture the imagination and intrigue.

A lovely and fluid wall painting shows the Kykkos icon, held aloft by two monks while two altar servers walk backwards before it, swaying frankincense burners in its path. Following in their footsteps, the twelfth century Byzantine Emperor Alexius I Comnenos trailed by a column of helmeted soldiers, raises his hand in a gesture of giving. The icon was a gift to Kykkos from the Emperor, in gratitude to a Cypriot monk who healed his dying daughter.

Like the constant stream of visitors and pilgrims, we make a tour of the arcaded and imposing premises, capturing images of the lavish and, at times, heart-stopping modern mosaics. Set in a blaze of gold, a serious Virgin, unfolding the formula to salvation, stands guard to one side of the entrance. Domed ceilings hold painted scenes of the Virgin and child. Flowing lines and floral designs encompass angels above while below, journeying Magi and shepherds point to the overhead star.

Renowned throughout the Orthodox world, Kykkos has been instrumental in maintaining Cyprus' Hellenism throughout centuries of foreign domination. That Archbishop Makarios entered the monastery as a novice at the age of twelve and rose to become its abbot before becoming the republic's first president, has added considerably to its prestige. Both the icon, known for its efficacy in answering prayers, and the Archbishop's tomb in a cave on Throni Hill, behind the monastery, continue to make Kykkos the premier pilgrimage place in Cyprus.

Sharing a dramatic origin, stemming from the discovery of a glowing icon of the Virgin, *Machairas* Monastery also shares magnificent views over the eastern foothills of the Troodos Hills. On this occasion bathed in an aura of light, the legendary icon is said to have been detected inside a cave by two hermits from Palestine in 1148. The Byzantine Emperor, Manuel 1 Comnenos ordered a monastery to be built on the spot. Following two fires – in 1530 and 1892 – the monastery had to be rebuilt. The venerated icon survived and protected by a silver shell, is now kept in the iconostasis of the church. We made a fleeting visit, adding some impressive angel portraits to a growing catalogue of heavenly scenes.

If we came away from *Agios Neophytos* Monastery with a sense of foreboding, we left both Kykkos and Machairas Monasteries with a sense of the wealth and formality of much visited religious sites. Then a metaphorical stairway took us to a breathtaking heaven. Our destination was the restored *Panagia Chrysorrogiatissa* Monastery. Its very name – Our Lady of the Golden Pomegranate – is steeped in an alluring combination of legend and history. The pomegranate fruit, being symbolic and the slang for breast, creates a fascinating and, on this island, not unusual link with the golden breasted goddess Aphrodite. In common with both Kykkos and Machairas, the monastery's foundation is attributed to a miraculous icon of the Virgin. Like the goddess, this icon is said to have floated over the sea and alighted on the shores of Pafos.

The story told is that in 1182, a number of hermits lived in the vicinity of Kremasti. One night, during the feast of the Assumption, one of the hermits, named Ignatius, saw a light in the distance. Intrigued, he went to investigate and came upon a glowing icon of the Virgin. On his return, he stopped to rest and had a vision of an angel, who instructed him to build a monastery in that very location. Ignatius told his fellow hermits; together they built a monastery, dedicated it to the Virgin and by common consent, decreed that Ignatius was abbot.

From the start, we fell in love with the monastery's rustic appearance; the way the building follows the curve of the land, now fronted by a similarly accommodating tarmac road. It survived both the Franks' attempts to convert Orthodox Christians to Catholic, and then the terrible oppression and pillaging of the Turks. Restored but not overly modernised, its appeal is reflected in a naturalness provided by its very lack of symmetry: overhanging wooden balconies, shaded walkways, lined with potted plants and, best of all, a sense of welcoming informality from portly, black-robed monks. Its artwork – icons and wall paintings, gold and silver engraved vessels and embroidered vestments – is there for those seeking to indulge further into the heritage of its monastic past.

Our self-indulgent visit was to photograph the monastery's outer rustic form and stunning mountain views, before sampling its famous wines. Then, just to let us know that things do not always go according to plan, we are halted in our tracks. On an archway over a porch, a wall painting of the Dormition of the Virgin grows before us.

Portrayed in sombre browns and greens, a faded and thought-provoking scene of haloed saints, sad eyes fixed on the Virgin's lifeless form, unfold. With memories still in mind of a modern rendering of the eastern Byzantine form of the Dormition at Kykkos, we are confronted by a different story. In the Kykkos rendition, the figure of Christ holds a child in his arms – a metaphor for the Virgin's resurrected body and soul – over her lifeless adult form. This Orthodox artist shows the adult Virgin, a smaller version of her lifeless form, hands lifted towards heaven, in the very act of ascending to the waiting figure of Christ. Meanwhile below, an angel is brandishing a sword over a lurking satanic figure. This artist appeared intent on making clear that Satan never gave up hope of collecting even the purest of souls – a reminder that art, like oral history, can tell different versions of the same event. Having captured the scene on film for later contemplation, we gravitate to the monastery's vine-covered trellis and prepare to sample the celebrated Monte Royia wines.

"*Kopiaste*," invites a kindly monk, with an impressive silver beard and smiling bespectacled eyes, as he hands us glasses of the selected dry white Agios Andronikos wine.

We learn that the monastery's abbot, Brother Dionysus, was appropriately named. After a lapse of forty-four years, he was responsible for putting the Monte Royia Winery back on its feet. We drink to his health and to heavenly views across sun-drenched, vine-covered slopes that unfold to a panorama of skyward reaching peaks.

When the melting sun slides below the treed horizon, we head once more for the beating heart of Pafos, the sun blessed golden city – on this occasion to meet up with friends from Dubai at *Komboloi* Taverna and Restaurant.

"Eat once and you will want to come again," promised Stavros Stavrinou, proprietor and chef de cuisine.

There is no doubt it that *Meze* is King. All we have to do is sit back and enjoy: grilled *halloumi* (goat's milk cheese), *kolokithakia* (courgettes), *tahine* (sesame dip), *koupepia* (stuffed vine leaves) and *lountza* (smoked pork marinated in red wine). As wine glasses are emptied and refilled, with none other than Aphrodite, the Goddess of Cypriot wines, dishes keep appearing. Our host grows merry and serenades us on his small bouzouki.

"Stavros," he croons. "S for star. F for flower. L for love."

It was Greek to me, but who needs sense on the Island of Love?

*****

Legends, traditions and stories concerning miraculous Theotokos icons said to have been painted by Saint Luke continued to intrigue. It is known that Saint Luke was a gentile, a native of Antioch in Syria and that he was a physician, enlightened in the Greek medical arts. It is also evident that he had a special connection with women in the gospel, especially the Virgin, and that he had keen narrative skills. It is in Saint Luke's Gospel that we hear of the Annunciation, Mary's visit to Elizabeth and the Magnificat – surely, the most memorable and lovely of prayers – as well as the Presentation in the Temple and the story of the disappearance of Jesus in Jerusalem.

For three hundred years of Byzantine rule in Palestine, Jerusalem had been a Christian city. Then, with the adoption of Christianity as the official religion of the Roman Empire, it became the centre of the Christian world. A direct result of the ensuing development and lavish spending was a flourishing of religious tourism and a trade in relics, including everything from the chains of Saint Peter, nails that fastened Christ to the cross, the cross itself, as well as paintings of the Virgin. This trade enabled the relics to reach Constantinople; very often they were transported via Cyprus, the closest stopping-off place or port of call en route to Europe, India, Russia, Syria and beyond – to places where miracles attributed to the icons are said to have occurred.

There is no hard and fast evidence that Luke was, or indeed that he was not an artist. That he was an artist with words is self-evident. His descriptions of the events in the life of Christ have become inspiring and favourite themes of Christian painters throughout the world. That icons of the Virgin associated with Luke may or may not be his artwork does not detract from the miraculous events witnessed and ascribed to them. These vary from dramatic accounts of the delivery of Russian monks and monasteries from the plundering raids of Mongol hordes, attributed to the icon of 'Our Lady of Vladimir', to quiet discoveries of glowing icons by saintly monks in Cypriot caves, once inhabited by hermits.

To this day, the monks in Cyprus continue the tradition of icon painting. In Stavrovouni Monastery, perched at 2,257 feet in the Troodos Range, icons painted by Brother Kallinikos are sought by collectors worldwide. From his studies in Athos in Greece, he has inherited the genuine Byzantine way of painting using tempera on linen over wood, liquid wax and oil, mixed with gold leaf, and he even makes varnish with turpentine from his own pistachio trees. A small Madonna and child will set you back three hundred Euros. Whether or not you can expect a miracle is not part of the bargain.

Footnote

Just weeks after our return from the 'Island of Love' Richard lost his life to cancer: a tragic and unexpected end to his 57 years and our shared journey in this life. It wasn't until some two years later when I met Jill, a similarly positioned and similarly minded friend that I felt able to continue with my travels. An expedition with the RSD Travel Ltd. 'On the Trail of the Crusaders' provided an opportunity for us to explore the foundations and history of Christianity in Northern Cyprus and Asia Minor – today's modern Turkey, the former homeland of Saint Paul – the area he visited on his first missionary journey.

Northern Cyprus

On the Trail of the Crusaders

An early morning wake-up call at the Premier Inn was preparation for an unsociable flight-time from Gatwick to Antalya in Southern Turkey. Accompanied by Jill and fellow travel companions, we were en route to Northern Cyprus. Since direct flights to Turkish occupied Northern Cyprus were not acceptable to the European Union a detour via Antalya was made – confirmation that diplomatic and commercial isolation of Northern Cyprus, continues to this day. When we finally arrived at Nicosia Airport we were met by Ibrahim, our guide and taken to a coach, to be transported to the Riverside Holiday Village at Alsancak, in the foothills of the Kyrenia Mountains. This was to be our accommodation for the first three nights of a tour: 'On the Trail of the Crusaders' before heading for Southern Turkey.

It didn't take long to discover that although the Holiday Village was situated on the side of a valley there was no sign of a river; the only indication of a river's former presence was a dried-up gully at the foot of the slope. In fact, such is the current shortage of water in the region that pipes transporting water from Southern Turkey have been laid across the bed of the Mediterranean Sea. A number of haphazardly placed modern apartment blocks, constituting the resort, straddle the slope overlooking the gully while an assortment of villas, belonging to local people, dot the opposite hillside.

Further research revealed that the original district of Alsancak filled a single ravine with runnels and aqueducts to irrigate lemon orchards, while olive groves and carob trees were interspersed with houses on the higher slopes. Furthermore, the Greek name for Alsancak, *Karavas* that came from the word *Karavai* meaning ship, referred to a former port on the coast that was frequently visited by sea going vessels. It was here that the Turkish navy landed, during their invasion in 1974, leading to the ongoing, unsettled political situation. One positive step forward was the opening of the border with southern Cyprus in 2003 – since then the northern coastal region has developed into a favoured tourist destination.

Once we had been directed to our plain but adequately furnished rooms our priority was food and drink. Our first task was to find the restaurant. A large signpost directed us to a footpath that ran alongside the ravine, before heading inland towards a more recent development of apartment blocks, where it diverged in various directions. Our quandary, about which path to follow was solved when a group of fellow travellers arrived and escorted us to a large buffet-style 'help yourself' restaurant.

*****

Mist and low cloud greeted us the following morning as we boarded a coach in readiness for a truly historic day: Visits to Saint Hilarion Castle and Bellapais Abbey, followed by Kyrenia Castle and Harbour. As the coach climbed into the foothills of the Kyrenia Range the cloud overhead began to break, revealing the jagged edges of the mountains' peaks; reaching to over 700 metres they marked the skyline like the ridged back of a mammoth dinosaur. The more traditional explanation of indentations between the peaks: *Pentadaktylos* – 'Five Fingers' – revives the legend of the Byzantine hero Digenes Akritas, whose fingers are said to have created the grooves when he grasped the ridge as he leapt from Anatolia to Cyprus to escape pursuing Saracens.

The coach continued its narrow zigzag uphill route, towards a first sighting of the remains of the castle wall, bringing its historic past to life. The legend told is that Hilarion, a seventh century hermit monk – believed to have sought refuge in Cyprus to escape Arab attacks in the Holy Land – lived in a cave in the Kyrenia Mountains. The monk's choice of this strategic position for his retreat – close to a pass through the mountains and overlooking the coastal plain – was recognised by the Byzantines as a place of refuge from further marauding Arab attacks. In the 11th century they built a monastery and chapel alongside the saint's tomb and converted the site into a castle. Richard the Lionheart captured the castle on his way to the Third Crusade – one of three Crusader castles, along the Northern Cyprus coastline that together with Buffavento and Kantara were used to defend the island from pirates and other invaders.

In the 13th century the castle fortress was taken over and turned into a military stronghold as well as the summer home of the *Lusignan's*: French ruling family. The three distinct levels of the castle fortress: the lower, middle and upper *enceintes* (walled enclosures) surrounded by tiers of towers and battlements, clinging to the mountain's precipitous sides, formed impenetrable sanctuaries and places to look out for invading enemies. When the Venetians took possession in 1489 the strongholds fell into disrepair and eventually became the ruin that they remain to this day.

Our journey continued up a hairpin trail with occasional glimpses of the remains of towers and battlements. It was the unexpected appearance of Turkish Flags, marking a military enclave that brought us back in time. From behind a barbed wire fence armed, lethargic soldiers watched us pass: a tangible reminder that in the 1960s the impregnable ruins became a look out base for Turkish Cypriot fighters. Finally, we arrived at a levelled parking space cut into the side of the mountain.

Warned of the steepness of the 'on foot' ascent, up a narrow pathway leading to the lower walled enclosure of the castle, some of the group opted to remain in the parking area and enjoy the panorama of extensive views. Putting aside concerns regarding a recent injury to my knee, incurred when playing tennis, I joined Jill and a handful of hardy travellers making for a stony track which led up a steep slope to a narrow entrance into an enclosed area, used mainly for soldiers and their horses to defend the castle when under attack. We paused to take in commanding views over buttressed walls, before ascending once again; finally, the track – punctuated by occasional steps – took us to and through an imposing Lusignan archway into the courtyard of the middle-enclosed area. My attention was immediately focused on two stone, carved corbels projecting from the outer wall: one resembled that of a dragon – the other a woman with flowing hair. The only explanation of their significance I could come up with was that they were symbols of imperial royal power and supreme authority representing King Peter 1: King of Cyprus and Queen Eleanor of Aragon.

BIZANS KILESI / BYZANTINE CHURCH, printed on a large signpost, guided us towards another grand archway and into the remains of the main body of the former church. Although roofless and empty, sunlight and shadows stirred memories of the saintly monk, as well as of those who had once lived and prayed in this remote location. It was time to record our visit on film. Two Turkish visitors had followed us through the archway; while one obliged by taking the camera, his friend posed alongside of us: a symbol, perhaps, of transient peace between previously warring nations.

Back in the courtyard we caught up with Ibrahim who was heading for another steep, rock-strewn path leading to the notorious Prince John's Tower. In 1373, warned that his Bulgarian bodyguards were plotting against him, Prince John of Antioch is said to have responded by taking them prisoner. On his orders they were then taken to the top of the tower where he had them thrown into the abyss below. Ibrahim led us through a narrow doorway and up the dark curving stairway on the inside of the tower then stopped unexpectedly; a barrier had been installed and further access was forbidden. Apparently, its state of disrepair made it too dangerous to continue. However, it was possible to take it in turns to look up to the top of the tower, where an image of a figure against the sky had been placed: a bleak reminder of the terrifying moment faced by each man before hurtling to his death. From an arrow slit in the tower wall, the view of the mountain's vertical, rock-strewn side took the breath away while the height and position of the tower, built on a crag some 732 metres above the plain, made its heart-rending history all too real.

We had just enough time to recover our breath when we found ourselves facing another set of steps: we were on our way to the Royal Apartments in the upper enclosure, built between twin peaks of the mountain. The highlight of these remains is the Queen's Window: the place where Queen Eleanor is said to have surveyed her kingdom. Extensive views across the foothills of the mountains to the coastal region also served as a lookout for invading enemies. It was a convenient place to rest and absorb the view as well as to contemplate the turbulent history of this fortress retreat before summoning the energy to begin the descent. As we followed the narrow trail down the hillside, my mind centred on the lives of those who had laboured to create the incredible battlements and towers in such treacherous conditions. Breathless once again, but more than satisfied with our expedition, we boarded the coach in readiness for more footsteps and shadows.

*****

Next on the agenda and high on my wish list of places to visit was the settlement of Bellapais, in the Pentadaktylos foothills. Lawrence Durrell's perceptive and fascinating account of his life here during the EOKA period – between 1953 and

1956 – had brought it to life for me. The spectacular setting of Bellapais Abbey – perched on the hillside, overlooking the Kyrenia plain and the azure blue of the Mediterranean Sea – as well as Durrell's 'Tree of Idleness' are the main attractions of this picturesque village. A huge placard marked the position of the tree standing in the village square, before the remains of the abbey walls: the place where Lawrence met and spent time relaxing with his neighbours. An arched gateway led to the abbey's 13th century church. Founded by the *Lusignan* ruler, Aimery, as *Bellapais*: Abbey of Peace, it was a place of refuge for Augustinian monks, fleeing Palestine. I paused to photograph traces of a lovely 15th century Italian fresco of the Virgin and child with a saintly figure alongside, over the arched '*Bitter Lemons of Cyprus*' entrance door. The church was locked but once again sun and shadows added to the air of the not forgotten past, this time in huge Gothic archways and columns rising from lemon groves: the remains from Ottoman raids of the former abbey.

I had a favour to ask of Ibrahim: To visit the place where Lawrence Durrell once lived. It so happened that the gods were on my side. Ongoing conflicts between the Turkish government and Kurdish insurgent groups, as well as recent Turkish /Russian hostilities had resulted in a drop in the number of tourists leaving Marie, an out-of-work local guide, free to join our group. Marie was more than happy to escort Jill and me up the narrow-cobbled street to where Durrell's former home overlooked the abbey and the sea. Although the house has been renovated, a yellow circular commemorative plaque remained nailed to the wall: 'BITTER LEMONS', taken from the title of the account of his stay, is printed at the top, while beneath an illustration of lemons over Kyrenia Harbour is printed: 'LAWRENCE DURRELL – LIVED HERE 1953–1956'.

Finally, a downhill route to historic Kyrenia; built round a beautiful harbour and horseshoe shaped wharf and flanked by the imposing walls of a castle: built by the Venetians in the 16th century over previous Crusader fortifications Kyrenia has become a favourite tourist resort. Cafes, restaurants and waterside terraces that have replaced former carob warehouses, offered a welcome break. Rejuvenated, we set off to explore the shoreline that offered perfect views of sections of the harbour and castle walls: Byzantine, Lusignan and Venetian remains combined to reflect a complex and much fought over past. The sun was out, sky and sea deeply blue providing a perfect backdrop to capture on film some aspects of the picturesque setting of this historic castle and port.

The nearby Ancient Shipwreck Museum in Kyrenia Harbour where a fourth century BC Greek Merchant Ship, from the time of Alexander the Great is on display provided a fitting end to a truly historic day. First discovered close to the harbour by a Greek Cypriot diving instructor in 1965, the remains were salvaged between 1967 and 1969. It is believed that the merchant ship was attacked and plundered by pirates. In spite of its age, the curved remains of the hull before us had been remarkably well preserved in the silt and mud of the seabed. Other finds included wine amphora from Rhodes and jars of perfectly preserved almonds. Millstones, used as ballast, lead net weights as well as wooden spoons, cups and dishes, once used by the crew, were further confirmation of Kyrenia's fascinating and uneasy past.

On our return to the Holiday Village members of the group were discovering various shortfalls in the amenities, especially an absence of hot water and plugs for washbasins. As it happened one shortfall came to the rescue of another: The drop in the number of guests made it possible for those of us with problems to move to accommodation where everything worked, enabling the travellers to focus on preparations for visits to the former powerful island cities of Salamis and Famagusta. The chequered history of this region, on the eastern coast of Northern Cyprus, is just as dramatic as that of Kyrenia in the west.

Salamis and Famagusta

The following morning, we set off to cross the Mesaoria Plain. That *Mesaoria* literally means 'Between the Mountains' describes its position between the Kyrenia range to the north and the Troodos range to the south. Travelling across the flat, low lying plain, between the mountains, was a potent reminder of the island's geological past: Twenty million years ago, Cyprus was two islands then, approximately one million years ago, the Mesaoria plain rose from the sea to join them. I still have warm memories of exploring the Troodos Mountains on a visit to southern Cyprus: hidden villages and monasteries tucked into valleys and foothills; invitations from friendly, welcoming monks to 'Kopiaste' – 'Sit down and share with us' – a glass of wine from vineyards that covered surrounding slopes.

There were no monasteries and kindly monks on the long haul from Morphou Bay on the west coast, to Famagusta Bay in the east – instead, our route was broken, at times, by intimidating Turkish military enclaves. However, our hearts and minds were set on a visit to a very special monastery – that of Saint Barnabas, just west of Salamis, the place of his birth. This was to be the starting point for further explorations in the footsteps of both Saints Paul and Barnabas: the time when Barnabas, accompanied Paul on his missions in Asia Minor in A.D. 45 and helped establish the Christian Church in Cyprus.

According to a local legend, Barnabas was stoned to death by Jews and buried secretly in a cave by his kinsman Mark. Some four hundred years later, when the church in Cyprus was threatened with absorption into the Apostolic Sea of Antioch, it is said that the Barnabas appeared to the Cypriot Archbishop to reveal his burial place. When the body was uncovered a handwritten copy of Saint Matthews's Gospel, found lying on his chest, was presented to the Byzantine emperor who responded by authorising church autonomy in Cyprus. The original fifth century building, destroyed by Arab raids was reconstructed with pillars and capitals in the 18th century. It now houses an icon museum as well as various archaeological relics.

We arrived to stand before an assortment of domes and curved rooftops sheltering the monastery walls and reflecting its Greek Orthodox past. While an impressive selection of iconic artwork is on display inside the museum, my lasting memory is of a series of uncovered original fifth century frescoes on the walls of the entrance. One shows the archbishop and monks standing over the saint's body with a copy of the Saint Matthew's Gospel on his chest; another has an image of Christ blessing the kneeling figure of the archbishop; then the emperor is depicted handing the archbishop a garment of office. Finally, he is shown wearing the purple cloak of office and carrying a sceptre. Our guided tour ended with a visit to the domed mausoleum that has been built over the final resting place of Saint Barnabas. Inside a holy water font stands beside a set of steps, leading down to his tomb: a sombre but memorable place.

On our way back to the coach we made a detour to pause beside a cluster of ancient rock cut tombs. Ibrahim gestured to the far side of the monastery where, he explained, a royal necropolis of giant-stone, tomb-chambers dating from the 7th and 8th centuries once held the remains of horses as well as chariots and slaves, sacrificed at the time of the royal person's burial, for use in the hereafter. Sadly, the overgrown site had been severely looted long before its discovery in 1957. A short coach ride later we drew up at the entrance to the former powerful Roman city of Salamis. Damaged by earthquakes and seismic waves the city was then restored by the Byzantines in the fourth century; re-named Constantia, after the

Emperor Constantius, son of Constantine the Great, it became the Christian capital of Cyprus until Arab attacks in the seventh century led to its demise.

It was good to stretch our legs as we made our way between lines of re-assembled columns past the Agora – public marketplace – and remains of the baths towards the Greco-Roman theatre. Apart from the theatre's impressive tiers of restored seats most of the site is overgrown; re-assembled pillars and broken paved walkways between incomplete low walls, helped to identify different sections. Nevertheless, with Ibrahim as our guide, it was an atmospheric place to explore and feed the imagination before heading for the ancient port of Famagusta. Ibrahim reminded us that the Crusaders, fled to Famagusta when they lost their last foothold on the coast of Palestine in 1291. Developed by the Lusignans as a port of call for Christian pilgrims heading to the Holy Land, it then grew in importance as a centre of trade under Genoese and Venetian merchants, as well as of Christianity and is reputed to have once had 365 churches.

Rain greeted our arrival alongside the imposing Venetian walls that held the Ottoman Turks at bay between 1570 and 1571. The highlights of our visit were the Citadel, standing out from the Venetian wall alongside the harbour – known as Othello's Tower it is said to have been used as the setting for Shakespeare's play, while nearby stands the former magnificent Lusignan Cathedral of Saint Nicholas – the place where the Kings of Cyprus received the Crown of Jerusalem. Taken over by the Turks it was converted into *Lala Mustafa Pasha Mosque*.

Given the weather conditions Ibrahim directed us to various cafes and bars before giving a time to meet for the homeward journey. While the majority of the travellers headed for the bars, Jill resolutely set off to walk along the harbour walls, while I decided to shelter under nearby trees to wait and hope for the rain to subside. The sky did finally clear allowing just enough time to capture the Citadel on film, as well as the triple sculptured portal and immense circular window of the cathedral's west façade; that one of the cathedral's twin towers was topped by a spiked minaret, was a further reminder of the ongoing invasive past.

Nicosia

Our final day at the Riverside Holiday Village was blighted when I inadvertently walked into the wooden corner at the end of the bed. The unprotected joint cut into the flesh over the shin, leaving a deep gash. From past experience I knew that it was important to see a pharmacist and keep the wound securely covered. Fortunately, our last day in Cyprus was to be spent in Nicosia and Ibrahim assured me that this would be possible.

Ataturk Square, the dropping off and pick up place was memorable for the monument dedicated to Mustafa Kemal Ataturk (Father of Turks), the founder of democracy in Turkey as well as for the number of buildings dating from the years of British rule: 1878–1960. Venetian walls surrounding the city were becoming a familiar sight, as were outstanding ancient cathedrals that had been converted into mosques. The 14th century French Gothic Cathedral of *Agia Sofia* (Saint Sophia) was converted into *Selimiye Mosque* before becoming a museum. Similar in style to Saint Nicholas Cathedral it was used for the coronation of Lusignan princes as kings of Cyprus; a second coronation in Famagusta followed to endow the honorary title of King of Jerusalem.

Worship practices and royalty were put aside for a speedy and successful visit to a helpful pharmacy before heading back to visit a caravanserai. This one was built by the Ottomans in 1572, a year after they seized Cyprus from the Venetians. As we entered a fortified gateway into the inner courtyard it was apparent that we were not alone in using this caravanserai as a stopping off place. Groups of students were gathered in various places across the square. I stood for a while taking in the quadrangle of beautifully arcaded cloisters. The architecture was a reminder of a passage 'In Xanadu' when Dalrymple points out that the use of the pointed Gothic arch dates back to the eighth century in the Islamic world and that, in all probability, Islam passed on this discovery to Europe through the medium of Norman Sicily. Thus, the origin of the pointed arch in European Gothic lay not in France, as I had believed, but in the Muslim world. Then as I focused on the small dome topping the hexagonal place for prayer within the courtyard, I recalled that the use of the dome is just one example of the Islamic adoption of Christian architecture; this dates back to the 4th century when Christian baptisteries and shrines were domed – such as the Lateran Baptistry and the wooden dome over the church of the Holy Sepulchre in Jerusalem. In the sixth century the Emperor Justinian made domed church architecture standard throughout the Roman East. His magnificent Hagia Sophia inspired copies for centuries to come.

Today rooms in the upper level of this caravanserai served as galleries and workshops while, the lower level consisted of a range of cafes and shops for visitors, whatever their belief.

This was our venue before heading for the airport and a return flight to Antalya for the next stage of our journey through the mountainous region of Southern Turkey *On the Trail of Saint Paul*, and the disciple Barnabas.

Southern Turkey

Pamphylia

'From Paphos, Paul and his companions sailed to Perga in Pamphylia...and when they had preached the word in Perga, they went down to Attalia. From Attalia they sailed back to Antioch, where they had originally been committed to the grace of God for the work they had now completed'.

Acts 13: 13 & 14 26

Through the missionary work of Paul and Barnabas, the former Roman province of Pamphylia – became one of the early centres of Christianity. Situated on a narrow coastal plain, at the foot of the Taurus Mountains, it was to be the location of our overnight stop.

Any sense of the past was lost as the coach headed through Antalya's busy, floodlit streets to our hotel. Fears of noise from non-stop traffic were quelled when we discovered that our rooms overlooked a grassy square, lined with trees. However, an early morning wake-up call from a local mosque put an end to the uninterrupted sleep we were hoping for before an expedition into the snow-clad mountains.

As the coach left the hotel and headed up a main street the mountains were there before us. Our target was the ancient city of Hierapolis and the nearby remarkable *Pamukkale*: a white wonderland of terraced pools and petrified waterfalls formed by hot mineral cascades that transform calcium carbonate into brilliant travertine terraces.

Within minutes the coach was climbing into the foothills of the mountains. Ibrahim explained that the mountain people suffered from a poor level of education and their income from farming was small. Lack of rainfall and shallow, stony soil meant low yields of the main crops of wheat, barley and chickpea as well as poor grazing for livestock – mainly goats, cattle and sheep.

Today, a good number have migrated to coastal areas to work in the hotels of the fast-developing tourist industry.

In William Dalrymple's[1] account of his travels, he describes Anatolia as the former *'Breadbasket of the Roman Empire that provided the backbone of the Byzantine army'*.

When the armies of the First Crusade marched through Turkey – only twenty years after the battle between the Byzantine Empire and the Seljuk Turks in 1071 – they found that many of the Empire's most fertile provinces were already waste. It was when the pastoralist Turks swept into the region that the fields were left untilled and the established irrigation systems broke down with the result that the land dried up. This was wholly evident from the stony, empty slopes surrounding us. Then a 'not to be missed' sign to the 'Tugba Restaurant' – on the doorstep of Pamukkale – was the signal for our first stop. Seated at tables on an outside terrace and surrounded by a panorama of snow-clad peaks, we celebrated our arrival with a glass of wine while waiting for the food to be served. Hierapolis: Sacred City was next on the agenda. Built by the kings of Pergamon, alongside the white terraced hillside of Pamukkale in the second century BC, this ancient Greek city's complex history includes its foundation as a thermal spa: doctors used the nearby healing springs as treatment for their patients. Under Roman rule a theatre, baths, a gymnasium and several temples were built. Its history in brief takes us into the footsteps of the apostles. Starting in the first century AD, through the influence of the apostle Paul a church was built here; it was also the place where it is said that the apostle Philip spent the last years of his life before being martyred. Then under the Byzantine emperor Justinian, the baths were transformed to a Christian Basilica.

Finally, during the reign of the emperor Constantine, the city became a bishopric and important religious centre for the Eastern Roman Empire. Ibrahim explained that the city had been repeatedly rebuilt following major earthquakes including the Thracian earthquake in 1354. The ruins were slowly covered with a thick layer of limestone. Thanks to the excavation work of Italian scientists, between 1957 and 2008, serious reconstruction of the site has taken place.

We made our way over the stony hillside and through the Frontinus Gate: the monumental entrance to the Roman city sporting elegant arches, flanked by two Hellenistic round towers. Ibrahim then briefed us on the layout of the site: a

---

[1] William Dalrymple: From the Holy Mountain

colonnaded pathway between columns and under arches led towards the remains of the baths and various temples as well as the giant-sized tomb chambers of the necropolis. The most remembered tomb is that of the apostle Philip, who came to Hierapolis to spread Christianity over 2,000 years ago. A *Martyrium,* (church) of an octagonal, circular or cruciform shape was alleged to have been built upon the place where the Romans murdered him. It wasn't until 2011 that a team of Italian archaeologists discovered the remains of another church built nearby. This is believed to have been his final resting place.

While Jill planned to explore the site before visiting the theatre, I decided to adopt a more leisurely pace along an outer pathway that overlooked the site and then continue uphill to overlook the theatre. Thanks to UNESCO and the restoration work of Italian architects it was well worth the effort: before me stretched forty-five rows of curved seats, facing a 300-foot façade.

First constructed during the reign of the emperor Hadrian, after the earthquake in A.D. 60, the theatre was rebuilt in the third century under the orders of Septimius Severus, only to be destroyed by further earthquakes in the seventh century. Not for the first time on my travels, the magnificent Roman theatre, fed the imagination with memories of those who had lived, loved and died in the incredible, not forgotten past.

There wasn't time to visit the nearby Archaeology Museum, built for the safekeeping of remaining artefacts recovered from the site. Among them are statues of Greek and Roman gods decapitated by Christians, as well as Christian saints decapitated by Turks. Memories of headless statues, decapitated by invading Arabs, in the Greco-Roman sites in Libya stay with me. Even without their heads the beautifully sculpted figures conveyed a tangible sense of the beliefs of those who once lived there.

At the time of my travels through Libya Gaddafi was still in power, the country under sanctions and tourism didn't exist. I visited the abandoned sites with a handful of fellow oil-industry employees. To this day, I remember standing before the magnificent and complete bronze, life-size statue of the emperor Septimius Severus at the entrance to Leptis Magna: the place of his birth and the place he returned to embellish after becoming emperor. It was time to leave memories of headless statues and emperors behind and make my way downhill to catch up with Ibrahim at the pre-arranged meeting place, before heading for the nearby moonscape, wonder of the natural world.

Pamukkale

In the 1960s, the hot springs of *Pamukkale* were widely publicised and became a major tourist attraction, known as 'Cotton Castle'. Hotels, built on the site, drained thermal waters into their swimming pools, while over-use of the terraces by tourists caused considerable damage. Rescued by UNESCO in 2008 as a World Heritage Site, the hotels, as well as a road that had been built across the site, were removed and restoration took place. The first impression of this white wonderland more than lived up to expectations: a plethora of wide, curved terraces descending the hillside looked as if they had been carefully carved from descending layers of melting snow. Ibrahim explained that it was permitted to remove one's shoes and wade through the therapeutic water of the upper level of the nearest terrace.

Leaving Jill and fellow travellers to take advantage of this opportunity I decided to walk along a pathway tracing the upper level to capture on film some images of this unique natural world.

A small idyllic hotel with an outside pool, guarded by palm trees and views up to the white terraced hillside was our overnight retreat. Sadly, there was no time to relax and enjoy the ambience of our surroundings. After a hasty breakfast we were on the road again: a visit to the 13th century Mausoleum – sanctuary and tomb of Mevlana Rumi was next on the agenda. A poet, theologian and instigator of the Whirling Dervish Ceremony – a ritual dance of communication with God before passing it onto mankind. Mevlana is revered by Muslims. I was interested to learn that in 1925 Kemal Atatürk, the 'Father of Democracy' in Turkey passed a decree declaring that the 'Whirling Dervish' be suppressed. Since 1926 the Turkish Republic has permitted the 'Whirling Dervish' to re-open their premises in Konya. Since then it has become a popular tourist attraction.

We made our way beneath the turquoise dome of the Mausoleum and followed a line of visitors past the tomb of Mevlana and onto the dervishes' cells, their library and the hall where they performed their dance: a unique tradition combining costume, music and movement leading to a trance-like state and communion with God. Reconciled with the notion of death, the dervishes cast aside a black cape symbolising the tomb, to dance barefoot in a long white tunic (the shroud) and camelhair turban (the tomb's headstone). The dancers spun round and round like heavenly spheres to celestial music, reaching a trance-like state – the right hand turned upwards to receive God's grace and the left hand down to pass it on to mankind. The performance of this ritual dance – a combination of music, costume and gesture to evoke communion with God was extremely moving and offered some compensation for the schedule of another late night and early start.

*****

Our return journey downhill through the Taurus Mountains towards the Mediterranean Sea and Antalya included a visit to a leather, jewellery and carpet factory. During his visit to Anatolia in 1989, Dalrymple's quest was to see first-hand an example of the ancient tradition of carpet weaving developed by nomadic tribes, who wove rugs with knotted pile as floor coverings in their tents. Such was the apparent decline in the cottage industry of this ancient craft that it took several days for Dalrymple to locate just one home with a loom in a mud-thatched house off the beaten trail, in the region of Siva.

On this occasion we were fortunate to have the opportunity to watch a demonstration of the process of silk being reeled from tiny and perfectly formed cocoons in preparation for weaving into carpets. As I watched and listened my mind switched from interest and wonder and then to sadness. This close up experience brought to mind Lawrence Durrell's notebook account of what happens when the cocoons are placed in boiling water to make it easier to unravel the silk: "Silkworms die with a dreadful crackling and sobbing and the noise of sinews being ground." Then the guide's explanation of the origin of the silk trade and its history in this region took over. It is believed that monks were the first to bring cocoons to Byzantium from China in A.D. 555.

Over the years the trade spread forming an ancient network of caravan routes on the Silk Roads, connecting East and West from China to the Mediterranean Sea. Anatolia was an important meeting place of the Silk Roads – one of which went south to Antalya.

In Peter Frankopan's extraordinary history of 'The Silk Roads', he explains that it was not just trade and conquest that flowed along these roads – so did disease. The most devastating was the Black Death, which ravaged Asia and Europe in the fourteenth century. Victims depicted in the Toggenburg Bible have the distinctive swellings that the Italian poet and correspondent, Boccaccio said could be the size of apples. As the demonstration and talk ended Jill and I followed directions to a restaurant to wait for those travellers who had been tempted to order carpets or purchase leather and jewellery items. We were more than happy when Ibrahim signalled for us to return to the coach for the last leg of our journey on the historic Silk Road to Antalya.

A parking spot in Republic Square was conveniently situated for a visit to the ancient harbour. Before doing so we decided to follow a narrow pathway that ran uphill close to the massive, defensive Roman and Byzantine walls that once encircled the town. As we neared the summit the sound of rushing water took us towards the cliff edge. There, before us a great fall of water, haloed by a rainbow, tumbled over the rock face down towards the sea. Mission accomplished we made our way down through a narrow street, lined with market stalls between restored Ottoman houses leading to the ancient harbour.

When we arrived, we were more than ready for refreshments at one of a number of small, virtually empty cafes overlooking the harbour before tackling the uphill route to the parking area for the coach. Before us yachts and boats, embellished with dramatic images of sea pirates were waiting to take visitors on excursions to historical places along the coast – a reminder of the days when pirates hid in this sheltered harbour waiting for opportunities to raid merchant ships and take people as slaves. It was also a reminder that it was from this very harbour that Paul and Barnabas set sail for Antioch after completing their first missionary journey.

The overnight hotel overlooked a busy street and an impressive, turreted Russian hotel on the opposite side. Our stay reached a crisis point when, on the following morning, a group of German tourists arrived as we were preparing to leave. The problem was a shortage of lifts. Each time we pressed the button for the lift it went straight past to another floor. Such was the delay that Jill and a handful of super fit companions resorted to carrying their baggage down several flights of stairs. Fortunately, those of us who were reliant on some assistance did finally manage to get on a lift in time to board our coach.

En route to the Long Beach Hotel for our final week in Turkey, we stopped off to visit SANDLAND: the annual 'International Sand Sculpture Exhibition' set on a beach in Antalya. The theme: 'Seven Wonders of the World and Mythology' featured giant sized sculptures carved by sand sculptors from all around the world. The range included famous sites like the Pyramids, the Roman Colosseum and the Taj Mahal, plus Viking Warships and Noah's Ark. The sheer size of the sculptures, towering over us, and the incredible artwork that captured the expressions and emotions on the faces of people and animals, were a tribute to such gifted artists.

We arrived at the hotel to find not only a long beach but also an extremely long hotel! However, our rooms were blessed with balconies and views across a complex of circular swimming pools to the sea. Sadly, it didn't take long to discover the downside: the pools were empty, and a busy road ran between them and the beach. In spite of the fact that Jill and I had rooms several floors up, opening the glass doors onto the balconies invited the invasive noise of non-stop traffic. On the whole the rooms were comfortable and well furnished. I was less happy about dangling, jewelled light fittings and a mirror that occupied the greater part of the wall opposite the bed. There was one light switch. When switched on, reflections of the jewelled lights in the mirror created a dazzling display; it was not the place of rest one hoped for after a day of travelling and exploring.

At an arranged meeting, with staff from the hotel, we learnt that Ibrahim was leaving us for another group. We were sad to say farewell. He had been an excellent guide in every respect: patient, highly educated and with a completely unbiased attitude regarding the history of places visited. The person chairing the meeting presented us with an option: we could spend the entire week at the hotel enjoying the facilities, plus as much food and drink as we wanted; the alternative was a choice of expeditions to places of historic interest, plus breakfast and an evening meal. There was no question about which option was taken by Jill and me.

A further surprise lay in store. As we filed out of the room a tag was fitted to each person's wrist. Apparently, this was to ensure that we were residents at the hotel when we entered the dining room. Feeling like a sheep tagged, ready for slaughter, as soon as I reached my room, I removed the tag and attached it to the strap of my handbag. Then as I turned off the lights and opened the curtains, I was surprised to see two brightly lit fairgrounds. They appeared to be positioned at either end of the long beach and were part of the hotel's amenities.

The entrance to the restaurant opened onto a walkway which led through the dining area's assortment of tables and chairs to a 'serve yourself' section: row upon row of metal containers, filled with a variety and assortment of ready cooked foods, stretched into the distance. After some further exploring, I came upon selections of meat, fish and eggs being cooked and served on the spot. This seemed to be the best option. I realised I'd made the right decision when I chanced upon a visitor who said he worked for 'Health and Safety'.

"Do not touch anything in the containers," he warned. "The temperature, plus the unknown time-length of storage means there's a strong likelihood they are full of harmful bacteria."

He lifted the lid of a nearby container to inspect the contents.

"You will die if you eat," endorsed a tall German who had stopped alongside of us.

"Zat is OK," he added pointing to some freshly cooked chicken legs. Then Jill made a timely appearance and escorted me to a counter with a display of fresh fruit and vegetables.

"Various cheeses and breads over there," she said.

With a plan of sorts in mind we collected plates and cutlery and set about selecting our first meal in the long restaurant at the Long Beach Hotel.

Breakfast of cereals, toast and fruit prepared us for a visit to the remains of the Greco-Roman city of Side. The ancient city's coastal position, overlooking a horseshoe shaped harbour, had made Pamphylia into a highly successful and prosperous centre for trade in olives and, since Side is translated as pomegranate, I presumed that pomegranates were included. However, once again a substantial part of the income came from piracy and trading in slaves. It was when the harbour began to silt up between the 7th and 9th centuries that the city was eventually abandoned.

Side's more recent history includes the development of a village, within the fortified walls, in the early 20th century. In the late 50s, when archaeological excavations were taking place, visitors were attracted to the region with the result that local people moved into the site and took over ancient stone houses turning them into shops selling traditional goods. Further rapid development of houses and hotels along the coastline followed. An account in a recent copy of 'The Guardian' newspaper described the growing number of beach hotels as being 'lined up like rosary beads'. To provide easy access to the coastal resorts, tarmac roads have been built across the site.

It was with some trepidation that Jill and I joined a handful of fellow travellers for the beginning of a tour of this invaded city. The final approach to and through the site, on a tarmac road, took us under a Roman bridge and then to a parking area overlooking the ancient harbour. The driver-cum-guide pointed us in the direction of Apollo's Temple. White fluted columns, topped by the remains of a former pointed, arched headstone, perfectly positioned overlooking sea and sky was a photo opportunity not to be missed. A speedy visit to the renovated theatre set into the hillside focused on the impressive remains of curved seating that once accommodated 15,000 people. Then we were on the road again and heading for a boat trip into the estuary of the River Manavgat.

A cold wind greeted us as we were directed to board one of a number of moored vessels, some decorated with the now familiar gruesome pirate faces. In spite of the wind, we chose to remain on the upper deck for better views. As the boat headed inland, a mosque with tall, slender minarets outshone apartment blocks and palatial hotels that lined the mouth of the estuary. Meanwhile, as the crew were taking orders for drinks and an onboard barbeque, we were becoming further acquainted with fellow travellers: among them Taff, a retired army officer and his friend Mike, a former RAF helicopter pilot – accompanied by Sue and Marie, their nursing wives. John, who worked in the archaeology department at the British Museum, was travelling with his partner, Simone.

Finally, George and Stanley added to the interesting mix. George had a strong Irish accent. When I remarked that he reminded me of the deacon at my church who had a similar accent, his response, 'Actually, I'm Father George', came as a complete surprise. His casual dress code gave no suggestion of his priestly role in life. "And Stanley," he said gesturing towards his travelling companion who was following the flight of a bird of prey through his binoculars. "He's my accountant. We're looking forward to following in the footsteps of Saint Paul – and Barnabas," he said. "I'm sure you already know, they carried out extensive missionary work in this region."

As we exchanged information about ourselves and the various footsteps and trails, we were following, the crew were serving us barbequed fish and glasses of cool white wine, adding to the air of conviviality.

Once the remains of the barbeque had been cleared away and the boat was heading downstream towards its mooring, our guide was preparing us for the final visit on the itinerary: a walk through Manavgat's narrow cobbled street, past the inevitable stalls selling local wares, to a café, owned and run by a friend. I discovered the downside to the café when I followed directions up a narrow iron staircase, open on one side, to what turned out to be a filthy loo. The lack of an outer supportive railing made the descent precarious.

Just minutes, after I reached ground level Simone, who was on her way down, slipped and fell. Such was the pain in her twisted foot and leg that an ambulance was called, and she was taken to the local hospital. Sue then told me that another traveller, in our group, had suffered a leg injury similar to mine at the Riverside Holiday Village. Unaware of the importance of keeping the wound completely covered it had become severely infected and she too, had been taken to hospital. It was a disconcerting end to an eventful day.

Set 250 metres high on a rocky peninsula jutting into the Mediterranean Sea, Alanya Castle has a splendid, defensive position. Re-built in the Seljuk era, on the ruins of Byzantine and Roman fortifications, the remains are surrounded and protected by 6.5 km of walls and include 140 towers. In the 19th century, after the area was pacified under the Ottoman Empire and the castle ceased to be defensive, numerous villas were built inside the walls. This, no doubt, has contributed to its remaining on the UNESCO World Heritage tentative list. Today, it functions as an open-air museum. The plan was to first explore sections of the remains on foot, followed by a boat-trip for an offshore viewing of its dramatic setting.

Dropped off at the entrance, alongside the 200 metre high Red Tower – at the start of the castle walls – we made our way up and towards the inner fortress. En route I stopped to photograph the small domed remains of the 11th century Byzantine church. Further sections, in need of a great deal of restoration, were difficult to identify. Our priority was to follow a crenelated wall that took us to the corner bastion, at the highest point of the peninsula. The tough, uphill climb, rewarded by splendid views overlooking the Mediterranean Sea, confirmed the castle's defensive position. It was also possible to look back across the peninsula to a walled enclosure where half a dozen, red roofed modern villas, built inside the walls, were bathed in sunlight. The downhill route to the parking area was less breath-taking and provided uninterrupted sightings of precariously positioned defensive towers and walled enclosures.

Highlights of the boat trip that followed were offshore views of the castle and its walls plus a visit to the *Damlatas* (Stone in Drops) Sea Caves. Discovered accidentally in 1948 by stone miners, the caves feature thousands of years old semi-crystallised, limestone formations that date back to the Permian Period. Their growing reputation as 'asthma cure caves' is attributed to the belief that high carbon oxide in the air is capable of curing respiratory complaints. As we drew alongside a headland of rock, we dismounted one by one and made our way in a single line into and through a narrow tunnel to a walkway, with a handrail on one side. The route led through interconnecting caves where numerous stalactites and stalagmites, orange/brown in colour, grew and dropped from the ceiling and rock walls. Occasional hidden lights served to emphasise the extraordinary formations surrounding us.

Finally, back on board we were entertained by two members of the crew. Keen to demonstrate their climbing and diving skills, as well as to line their pockets, they were making their way up the slippery, precipitous rock face before diving into the turbulent water: a demonstration that was aptly rewarded. A feast of fresh trout, at an upmarket restaurant in Antalya Street-market, was a fitting end to our expeditions.

*****

A day of well-earned rest was on the cards. A walk round the hotel's, about to be filled, swimming pools for the start of the tourist season took us past shops, a tattoo studio and a disco parlour to a tunnel built under the road to provide access to the beach. A row of palm trees, beach huts and waves rolling onto the beach deadened the noise of traffic. We found a shaded spot to settle: Jill to read and me to catch up on my notes about the trip. Then, from time to time, as the tide came in and waves broke upon the shoreline, our attention was taken by sudden explosive sounds. Jill's curiosity was such that she went to investigate.

"Electric cable," she reported. "Running along the beach – sudden explosions of light when the waves break on joints where cables meet. Explains the sounds I heard from the balcony of my room," she added. "What's more, there's no seaweed or signs of life. I did see a large black pipe, following a breakwater into the sea. Goodness only knows what it's releasing!"

It all added up to the increasing sense of the lack of health and safety that we were now becoming accustomed to. Some compensation was made when, on our return through the tunnel we found that the swimming pool had been filled. Cold water kept me at bay but not my hardy companion. Heads attached to well-endowed bodies, spread on sunbeds lining the pool, were raised at this unexpected launch of the tourist season at the hotel.

*****

Manavgat Canyon – also known as the Green Canyon – situated between folds in the Taurus Mountain, was formed when a hydroelectric power plant was constructed across the River Manavgat. The scenic canyon is now high on the list of places to visit by boat in Southern Turkey. Our tour began with a coach trip into the foothills of the mountains: a zigzag route through lovely, pine-covered hillsides then downhill, unnervingly close to vertical cliff walls. We arrived to find the tide out, the boat anchored several metres offshore and a number of men pulling a large floating board to bridge the gap. This appeared to be the only means of embarking. With nothing to hang onto, it took some effort to remain upright on the sloping, slippery board. Then, with the help of the occasional outstretched hand of men on guard, everyone made it and the boat set off heading upstream through sparkling green waters, between rocky headlands. From time to time the gap between the now precipitous canyon walls grew unnervingly narrow and the sides more rugged. Trees grew from hollows in otherwise vertical slopes. Great falls of water tumbled over rocks. Sun and shadows added to the dramatic, scenic setting.

On this occasion there was no onboard barbeque, but we were heading to a riverside restaurant for lunch. We were soon to discover that not only was the restaurant beside the river but over it too! Once the men had secured the boat by ropes to a cliff-side rock, we disembarked and started to climb a series of steps that led up the steep side of the hill. I counted 144.We soon found that holding onto the loose metal railings, on the outer edge, was less safe than keeping close to the inner wall. The reward: a restaurant perched on a levelled area, cut into the side of the cliff with splendid views down to the canyon.

It wasn't until I made my way through the restaurant then along a small pathway, to capture some images of the canyon on film, and looked back, that I saw that a section of the dining area, where Jill was enjoying the remains of her lunch, extended beyond the cliff wall. I hurried back to tell her that apart from some stone supporting pillars, there was nothing but air beneath the wooden floorboards where she was seated. It was time to make our way down the hillside to the waiting boat.

Two further surprises awaited us when we arrived back at the hotel. Not for the first time a flood of German tourists had arrived. This resulted in long queues for 'on the spot' cooked food, plus a dramatic increase in noise levels in the low roofed restaurant. Then, a perfect ending to an eventful day: an invitation from Father George to share in a celebration of mass in his room.

*****

Thunder, lightning and heavy rain provided a wake-up call the following morning. Undeterred by the weather Abdul, our guide for a visit to the ancient Greco-Roman city of Perga, was waiting in reception.

"Hurry," he called. "Minibus waiting. Hurry," he added, "before Germans!"

As we made our way into the forecourt towards the minibus we passed a group of Germans standing and smoking alongside two waiting coaches. Others were forming a queue ready to board. Then, just minutes after our hasty departure the rain stopped, and Abdul was reminding us of the history of the ancient site. This included the Indo-European meaning of Perga: 'High Place' – referring to the acropolis, built on a hill, at the northern end. With its natural enclosed but now silted up harbour, Perga had been an important trading centre in Pamphylia. He then warned us that the theatre was currently under extensive restoration and closed to visitors and that our tour would begin at the horseshoe shaped stadium that once seated 12,000 spectators for chariot and foot races.

Out of the coach we met up with Father George and Stanley who were excited at the prospect of walking along the same colonnaded streets where Paul and Barnabas had once walked, at the start of their missionary work in Pamphylia in A.D. 46. They were also keen to see the remains of the Byzantine Basilica that had been built in Perga when Christianity was established.

The stadium was huge with remaining sections of curved seating built over a series of arcades where a complex of taverns and shops once stood. When we had finished exploring Abdul led us to the remains of the twin towers of the Hellenistic gate that marked the start of the colonnaded street leading into the city. Pointing to the decorative marble relief at the top of a nearby column, he explained that marble had been used throughout the city, even on the surface of the street.

"In places," he said, "it is possible to make out ruts in the marble, worn by wagon wheels!" He then went on to explain that wet, twisted strands of silkworm-silk had been used to cut the marble. The knotted silk rope was attached to two large wheels, powered by a giant water wheel. The silk rope was lowered onto the marble below, slowly cutting as it spun; the twisted threads were strong enough and durable enough to cut through the stone. Abdul then directed us to a clearly marked route along the colonnaded street that would take us to the Nymphaeum Fountain at the foot of the Acropolis as well as to the Basilica and Thermal Baths. With this incredible further information about the use of tiny silkworms' silk in mind we set off to explore.

From my research I knew that when Paul, accompanied by Barnabas and John Mark arrived in Perga on his first missionary journey John Mark, a native of Jerusalem, who was unfamiliar with Asia Minor decided to split from them and return to his homeland. Nevertheless, Paul and Barnabas did succeed in sowing the seeds of Christianity on their first and return visits. Perga became a Christian centre under Constantine the Great (324–337) – then from East Roman times the city became a bishop's residence. Three basilica churches were testimony to the success of Christianity. It was in the Byzantine era when the nearby River Cestus sanded up, followed by Arab pirate attacks in the seventh century that the inhabitants moved out and the city went into decline. Earthquakes and flooding then left the ancient city in ruins. In the early 20th century local people started using the ruins as building materials. Today, evidence of a massive restoration programme in progress was all around us.

With a plan of the site in hand we made our way along a colonnaded street to a place from where we overlooked an overgrown area to the remains of the Byzantine Basilica that became the seat of the Bishop of Perga and finally a Byzantine agora – meeting place. With its Corinthian columns and some mosaics still in place it was impressive. At its centre a round building is believed to be a temple dedicated to the ancient Greek God, Hermes.

Compared to other ancient sites that we had visited Perga did not live up to my expectations. This was partly due to the absence of statues of emperors and deities that add considerably to the sense of history of ancient sites – now in a museum in Antalya – plus the extensive restoration work that was underway. This, however, brings hope for the future of this ancient city.

The plan for the afternoon included lunch at a restaurant overlooking the renovated Roman bridge that crosses the Eurymedon River, followed by a visit to Aspendos: the 'Jewel in the Crown' of Greco-Roman theatres in the southern region of the Mediterranean in Turkey. What set this occasion apart was that not only had we arrived 'before Germans' but there was a complete absence of other visitors. The utter quiet in the deserted theatre echoed with memories of its historic past and brought our travels through Turkey to an equally memorable end.

Back at the hotel, in the throes of packing in readiness for a 1.30 a.m. flight from Antalya to Gatwick, I received a text message from my daughter:

'News. Bomb in Ankara. Are you OK?'

It was time to say farewell to Turkey.

Afterword

In the nine months following our return to the UK eleven further terrorist attacks took place in Turkey; in addition, nine suspected accomplices of suicide bombers, who killed thirty people in Istanbul, were charged with membership of an illegal organisation. The situation reached crisis point when, on December 20th the Russian Ambassador was shot dead by an armed Turkish police officer in Istanbul. The year ended with the shooting of another policeman in Istanbul on New Year's Eve, followed by a further shooting dead of thirty-nine people in a nightclub. The British Foreign Office warned against all but essential travel to Turkey.

Then just three days after the murder of the ambassador in Turkey, a Libyan plane was hijacked in Malta. We were relieved to learn that the attack ended peacefully when the hijackers – armed with pistols and a hand grenade – surrendered to the police. All 118 passengers disembarked safely from the aircraft. The men claimed to be 'pro-Gaddafi' supporters, escaping from ongoing factional political violence since his assassination in 2011 and requested political asylum in Malta.

I first visited Malta in 1993. I was on my way to Libya where I had accepted a teaching position to prepare the offspring of oil employees for entrance to UK universities. It was a time of extreme tension when, as a result of Gaddafi's failure to hand over the Lockerbie suspects the UN had tightened sanctions and the only access to Libya was by ferry from Malta or by air and road via Djerba Island in Tunisia. Apart from embassy staff, oil company employees were the only foreigners allowed into Libya. Memories of the horrors of the over-crowded night-time ferry crossing from Malta to my posting in the suburbs of Tripoli were overshadowed by my exit: deportation as a CIA suspect.[2]

News of the recently hijacked plane and a Libyan waving the Green Flag – a symbol of 'Green Resistance': A term used by sympathisers to pro-Gaddafi militant groups – was a potent reminder of the continued unrest in this war-torn country as well as Malta being a priority place still to be visited in order to complete our journey.

---

[2] *'Kiss The Hand You Cannot Sever'*, Melrose Books

Cappadocia

On the Trail of the Apostles

Tempted by the promise of a 5 Star Cultural Tour of Cappadocia, 'On the Trail of the Apostles' with RSD Travel Ltd. – enhanced by a display of photographs of hot-air balloons gliding over tufted hillocks, hiding ancient Christian settlements – despite news of bomb attacks in Ankara it was another opportunity not to be missed. As soon as Jill agreed to join me, we made our reservations. An out of season booking in early March, meant lower prices and fewer tourists. We were soon to learn that it also meant unsociable temperatures and flight times.

Having survived the journey from Gatwick to Antalya followed by a massive thunderstorm and a dawn awakening call from the local muezzin, at an upmarket coastal hotel, we boarded a coach with fellow travellers and prepared ourselves for a visit to the Roman theatre of Aspendos. We were now following on the trail of our own footsteps, from a previous visit to this historic place with the added advantage of being updated on the city's fascinating past by Richard our historian guide.

Situated alongside the previously navigable Eurymedon River, some 16 km inland from the Mediterranean Sea, the city of Aspendos was a prosperous centre for trade in Pamphylia in the fifth century BC and derived great wealth from marketing salt, oil and wool. To this day its main attraction is the Greco-Roman theatre. Built under the instruction of the Greek architect Zenon, in the reign of Marcus Aurelius (161–180), it underwent a decline in the late Roman and Byzantine periods. Taken over by the Seljuk Turks in the 11th century the theatre complex was used as a *caravanserai* (safe roadside inn for travellers): Its fortified, defensive position: a horseshoe-shaped *cavea*, constructed against a hillside, plus its barrel-vaulted sub-structure and solid outer walls, highlighted the danger of attack it faced from invading settlers and traders. Today, the restored theatre's reputation of being one of the best-preserved examples of 'eastern' Roman theatre construction in the world was apparent from the moment we arrived.

Escorted by Richard, we entered through an arched doorway that opened to a walkway and then up a series of steps between curved seating – estimated to have accommodated up to 20,000 visitors – and into a colonnaded gallery, surrounding the uppermost row of seating. When we were all assembled, Richard updated us on the theatre's complex, not so glorious past of gladiatorial events in the Roman era to the more cultural events of the present day.

"It's thanks to Mustafa Kemal Ataturk – the father of democracy in Turkey – that the theatre continues to be a major tourist attraction," he added. "When Ataturk visited the abandoned site, in the 1930s, he decreed that the magnificent structure should be a 'living' theatre dedicated to bringing the arts to the people. Thanks to him concerts, operas and ballets, which take place in late spring and early summer, are popular and well attended."

Before Richard had finished speaking a number of tour groups had arrived and were on our heels. Nevertheless, such is the size and grandeur of the restored theatre once again it was an atmospheric place to explore.

Next on the itinerary was a visit to the nearby Roman aqueduct system. The impressive remains of the tower-like structure that rose before us – preserved to a height of 100 ft – transferred water some 19 km from the Isaurian Mountains into a sealed siphon, while sections of bridges and tunnels that once carried the water across low-lying land marked the route to a second tower, on the outskirts of the city. Leaving the aqueduct, we headed for the equally impressive, restored Roman Bridge that crosses the Eurymedon River. Reconstructed by the Seljuk Turks in the 13th century, it remains an important link connecting the road that winds from the coastal region of Pamphylia to the Pisidian hinterland. Local people were well prepared for visitors; rows of stalls had been set up alongside the pathway, close to the bridge, making it difficult to get 'people-free' shots of the imposing arches.

Back on the coach we were more than ready for lunch but not so happy about the rather downtrodden restaurant that we were approaching. First impressions were deceptive. The architecture and décor, including a bamboo cane ceiling, were that of an original dwelling; the food was excellent and its location, set alongside the river, meant we were able to enjoy watching local fishermen hauling in nets full of fish.

****

On the following day, joined by Clara – a local guide – we boarded a coach to head inland on a journey of some 320 miles through vineyards and apricot groves then up and through the rugged Taurus Mountains before crossing the featureless Anatolian Plateau. The road looped and twisted between jagged, high reaching, snow-covered peaks – the sides littered with precariously balanced boulders; at times, it swung breathtakingly close to vertical slopes that dropped into unseen depths below. On this occasion, as on the rest of our tour, we were blessed with a careful driver. While other road users were intent on overtaking on steep slopes and hairpin bends, our driver kept a steady and secure pace. Meanwhile Clara had no qualms about safety but stood at the front of the coach, microphone in hand, to give detailed accounts of the history of Turkey – with interludes of 'amusing' tales from her travels.

At the foot of the mountains lies the ancient capital of Konya, one of the greatest Christian Communities at the time of the Apostles. While Peter established the first apostolic church outside of Palestine in Antioch (Antakya), it was in this very region that the disciples were first called Christians as they prepared to spread their belief. That Paul and Barnabas had followed a similar route to the one that we had taken from the coastal plain via Aspendos and through the Taurus Mountains – over a stony track, on foot and by donkey – at the start of their first missionary journey was testimony to the strength of their determination and belief.

Next on our agenda was a visit to the 13th century Mausoleum – sanctuary and tomb of Mevlana Rumi. A poet, theologian, Sufi mystic and instigator of the Whirling Dervish Ceremony, Mevlana is revered by Muslims. I was interested to learn that in 1925 Sufism was banned in Turkey by the new Turkish Republic. In 1926 Ataturk ordered that the Mevlana dervish lodge be turned into a mausoleum. We made our way beneath the turquoise conical drum and dome of the Mausoleum and followed a line of visitors past the tomb of Mevlana 'our leader', dervishes' cells, their library and the hall in which they performed their ritual dance, leading to communion with God. It was dark and highly decorated but with a quiet and respectful sense of a holy place.

The final stage of our journey ended at Kapadokya Lodge – our resting place in Nevsehir. Inside the front entrance my attention was immediately taken by a painting of a turreted fortress that covered the greater part of one of the reception walls. It appeared to have influenced the architectural design of the lodge. A further inspection of the frontage of the building: a series of square turrets with small inset square windows – the colour of the walls too, varying from light coloured stone at the front to a darker tone on the higher turrets at the back – confirmed this remarkable resemblance. On a nearby wall, alongside a painting of a rock-cut settlement, hung a fresco of the crucifixion which looked as if it had been cut and taken from its original location in one of the caves, used by Christian communities driven underground to escape persecution from Seljuk Turks. Frescos apart, the Lodge – a characterful and comfortable place – was to be our retreat for the next three nights, after days spent exploring ancient cave settlements and churches of the Christian communities in Anatolia.

The following morning, we crossed a volcanic plain to a cave dwelling in Sarati. Nothing had prepared me for this surreal landscape of tufted, snow-dusted pinnacles; formed when the ash from volcanoes solidified into a layer of tuff. Sculptured by wind, rain and snow into pillars, topped by dark, rock caps – they resembled giant-sized mushrooms. At times they appeared to have taken on the shape of creatures. My camera focused on the outline of two camels. Hence the region was known as 'Camel Valley' while a nearby complex of hillocks, converted into retreats by local Christians, was christened 'Fairy Chimneys'. Small windows had been cut into the rock walls of the upper storeys, while steps leading to arched doorways marked entrances to the lower levels.

As we left the coach ice cold winds and snow took hold. Fortunately, both Jill and I were prepared: hoods up and gloves on, we followed the guide up a set of worn steps leading to the entrance of a nearby hillock. A narrow tunnel led to an open area with niches cut into the rock walls. We knew that the settlement had once consisted of seven stories and that cattle were kept at this, the lowest level; pointing to a large boulder with a hole through the centre the guide explained that the stone was used to block the entrance. The hole was a lookout and, if necessary, a place through which to fire arrows at intruders. Once again worn steps took us to a narrow tunnel that led to the upper levels but since these were no longer safe to explore, we were directed to an exit to be greeted once again by snow-laden winds.

My excitement at the news that next on the itinerary was a visit to a cave retreat and monastery, used by the Orthodox Saints Gregory and Basil, was short-lived. The retreat had been converted into a hostel and coffee shop. It transpired that before UNESCO set up preservation terms in Cappadocia, a number of ancient sites had been taken over or built upon by the Turks. Now that organised tourism has taken hold, providing work and income for local people, the Turkish Government is not only complying with UNESCO Heritage Site rules but also laying claim to ancient sites they had previously appropriated or closed, by placing the Turkish flag alongside or before each of them. Taking photographs without the intrusive flag was a challenge. Weather conditions too, were not conducive to capturing the fascinating tufted landscape of this unique place at its best.

The day ended with a visit to a traditional carpet-weaving factory – the centuries old craft of hand-woven carpet making from wool and pure silk; this time-consuming craftwork was placed entirely on the shoulders of the young girls and women of the region. Following a lengthy talk and display of carpets, the focus of my interest moved from a woman demonstrating the painstaking hand-weaving carpet technique to a National Geographic photograph of a 2,500-year-old knotted carpet from an ice-tomb in the Altai Mountains. The *Pazyryk,* as it is known – said to be the oldest Gordian knotted carpet – is on display in St Petersburg Hermitage Museum.

*****

The highlight of the following day – and indeed of the trip – was a visit to Goreme Valley Museum. Countless 10th and 11th century rock-cut churches and monasteries carved into the snow-dusted pinnacles, hillocks, and frontage of sheer cliffs were there before us. The dominant image in the dome of each Cruciform church depicts Christ *Pantocrator* – All Powerful – reigning over the Archangels; others representing more conventional themes have a simple cross or ritual symbol. Among those we visited, the 10th century Church of the Buckle's well-preserved frescoes took the breath away: painted against a brilliant blue background in the apse and over the altar they included the Passion, Crucifixion, Entombment and Resurrection of Christ. Who were these uncelebrated, gifted artists? How deep was their courage, as well as that of the early Christians willing to risk their lives for their belief?

Surviving wall paintings in the Dark Church vary from the sixth century depicting John the Baptist to votive crosses and an angel worshipping the cross. When the actor David Suchet visited Cappadocia, as part of the BBC Documentary 'In the Footsteps of Saint Peter' his spontaneous reaction, when standing before frescoes in the Dark Church: 'Never have I seen anything like this!' was further confirmation of the stunning beauty of the artwork before us. And so, it continued. The 11th century Church of the Serpent was named after a fresco of Saint George and Saint Theodore on horse-back – Saint George is shown thrusting a spear into a snake, representing evil forces. A life-size image of Constantine the Great and the Empress Helena holding the True Cross was a tribute and a reminder of their importance and place in the history of both Constantinople and Jerusalem.

The fresco brought back memories of my visit to the Church of the Holy Sepulchre and the importance of Constantine the Great and the Empress Helena in the building of the church.

In the 4th century AD Constantine and his forces are said to have had a vision of a cross in the sky, with the words 'In this sign conquer' beneath it. Constantine's response was to have the symbol of the cross marked on his soldiers' shields, to sign the Edict of Milan, legalising Christianity throughout the Roman Empire and to send his mother, the Empress Helena to Jerusalem to look for the position of Christ's tomb. On her visit the empress discovered a relic of the cross on which Jesus was crucified, close to the rock-cut tomb where he was buried. Constantine then oversaw the clearing of the site and the building of the original church to enclose both the tomb and the place of crucifixion.

Over the years the church suffered destruction, deterioration and rebuilding. In the 12th century the Crusaders had the church restored. The present building, dates mainly from 1810. Since then it has continued to attract visitors and pilgrims worldwide.

Of more immediate interest was the discovery of inscriptions, located in the cornice and the north apse, inferring that Constantine and his son Leon were patrons of the artwork and responsible for funding the artists for the entire decoration within the church. Finally, the simply decorated Church of Saint Barbara remains memorable for the saint's tragic death: she is said to have suffered execution, by her father for converting to Christianity. Legend has it that, in retribution for his crime, her father was struck by lightning.

This truly memorable day was brought to a close by attending another Whirling Dervish ceremony. Once again, it was a moving spiritual and dignified presentation. It was also a reminder of Rumi Mevlana, the founder of the Dervishes, and our visit to the Mausoleum.

On our way back to the hotel Clara explained that on the following day we had the option of either taking advantage of a ride in a hot air balloon over Cappadocia's amazing volcanic landscape or we could have a day of rest at the hotel. If we were opting for the hot air balloon ride, we were asked to sign our names on the sheet of paper she was holding.

As a result of a recent report in the Daily Telegraph of a hot air balloon crash in Cappadocia: one person was killed and another critically injured, plus reports of previous crashes and deaths, concerns about safety standards had grown. While a handful of the group were prepared to take the risk of a possible accident, both Jill and I, along with other similarly minded travellers, decided to put safety first and to forgo this otherwise tempting expedition. A day of rest at the hotel was on the cards before heading once more across the Anatolian Plateau towards the Taurus Mountains.

The Silk Road

As we boarded the coach on the following morning Clara reminded us that we were travelling on the Silk Road to Antalya – an ancient network of trade routes through the Asian continents, connecting West and East from China to the Mediterranean Sea. This historic route was punctuated by Medieval Caravanserais: fortified hostelries that guarantied merchants a safe night's rest on the trade route linking Anatolia with Arabia and Mesopotamia. It was evident that we were no longer travelling in the 'On the Trail of the Apostles' but were now on the trail of Seljuk merchants and traders. The road took us past Aksaray and towards Konya en route to *Sultanhani*. Considered to be one of the best-preserved caravanserais (*hans*) of the Seljuk period and one of the most important stops on the caravan routes in the Middle Ages it was to be our first stop.

From my research I knew that although the Seljuk Turks did not invent the *hans* they were the first to build a planned network along their trade routes; ideally there was a caravanserai every eighteen miles – the distance it took a laden camel to travel in a day.

One minute we were crossing a featureless plain then what appeared to be a massive fortress was looming out of the distance. In William Dalrymple's account of his travels '*In the Footsteps of Marco Polo*' on the Silk Road in the late 1980s, he stops at the oasis village of *Sultanhani*: a complex of ancient mud brick farms with walled gardens – named after the nearby *han* by Seljuk Sultan Keykubad in 1230. Of royal foundation the *han* was apparently, deliberately built to make other caravanserai look small and indifferent.

As we drew alongside the imposing walls Clara looked at her watch. "Thirty minutes," she indicated. "We have to cross the mountains before dark." My immediate mission was to capture on film some aspects of the splendidly ornate Seljuk stone carving round the arched portal door. This achieved I then proceeded to distance myself in order to capture the sheer size and solidity of a section of the outer walls. Measures taken to prevent attack from bandits and intruders included heavily buttressed walls built from volcanic stone and similarly buttressed iron doors.

Mission complete, I was just in time to catch up with Jill and follow our group through the entrance door into a huge courtyard and then beneath one of a number of arched openings into a section that had been converted into a café for visitors. It was a dark and sombre place with a low stone ceiling and surrounded on each side by wide arches leading onto walkways that once led to dormitories and workshops as well as to a great stable hall for the safe keeping of camels and horses. Clara led the way to an area with benches covered with woven drapes, arranged round a low table then signalled for us to follow her under one of the archways to a self-service area to help ourselves to refreshments.

Sitting in the ancient caravanserai revived William Dalrymple's account of his visit; he describes it as empty as a ruined abbey and recalls the French author and diplomat Chateaubriand's nineteenth century description of Turkish merchants seated cross-legged on carpets, their needs attended to by slaves plus, other travellers smoking pipes, chewing opium and telling stories while camel drivers lay snoring on the floor. Today, apart from the section that had been prepared for visiting tourists, the caravanserai remained empty nevertheless it retained the sense of a cool, safe and solid retreat for those long-distance tradesmen of the not forgotten past.

The promise of a night's rest in another five-star hotel helped weary travellers prepare for and survive the last lap of the return journey through the Taurus Mountains. The downhill route to the hotel was even more hazardous than the uphill journey but once again our careful driver ensured our safety. Recovery time was short-lived.

An early morning start to the final day was spent largely on the trail of Turkey's craft traditions: visits to leather and jewellery workshops, including talks and displays to promote sales took care of the morning. The highlight of the day was a walk through the old settlement of Antalya where a statue of Attalus 11, King of Pergamon, the founding father of Antalya (Attaleia) around 150 BC, competed for my attention with a six-metre high, bronze statue of Ataturk, the founder of modern Turkey. Seated on a rearing horse, one arm extended in a gesture of peace and tolerance he is flanked on either side by a boy and a girl representing the youth of the nation.

The statues also heralded the approach to the former Roman port we had previously visited where the remains of towering walls guarding the harbour were reminders of Antalya's complex history and that the city reached its peak of prosperity as an important trade centre, under the Romans in the second century AD. It was a fitting place to end a remarkable journey.

*****

The unexpected discovery of a five-day Mediterranean cruise with Celestyal Cruises that included guided tours of Ephesus and Rhodes was a further opportunity to continue our journey *On the Trail of Saint Paul*. I was especially interested to learn that Saint Paul spent the better part of three years in Ephesus preaching the gospel and gaining many followers. Rhodes too was visited by Paul on his return journey to Jerusalem. The island also became a stronghold for the Knights of Saint John when they lost their foothold in Cyprus. Both Jill and I decided to take the opportunity to book 'out of tourist season' places in late October.

From my research I had been fascinated to learn that in the course of extensive excavations being carried out at Ephesus a cave on the slope of the Bulbul Mountain was discovered in 1892 by a group of Lazarist priests, who were looking for the tomb of The Blessed Virgin Mary. Known as the '*Kryphi Panaya*' meaning 'Hidden Virgin' the cave was believed to have been the place where, for her safety John brought the Virgin Mary to live, after the death of Jesus. However, other sources, such as 'Transitus Marie', describe her death and burial as taking place in Jerusalem. In more recent years – due to the number of Christian frescoes and inscriptions discovered beneath plaster on the walls of the cave, depicting not only Mary but also Saint Paul and Saint Thecla (a female disciple of Paul) the cave was renamed the 'Grotto of Saint Paul'. It is believed to have been a place of safety where Paul and early Christians gathered and prayed.

Furthermore, according to the *Acts of Saint John by Prochorus* written (160–70) by Lecius, the Evangelist John went to Ephesus at a very advanced age – after Mary's death in Jerusalem. Two letters, written about 370 state that the Blessed Virgin passed the remainder of her days in Jerusalem – that of Dionysius the Areopagite to the Bishop Titus (363) and the treatise *De transitu* B.M. *Virginias* (fourth century). To this day it remains a complex and contending history.

Nevertheless, two further buildings in the region of Ephesus are dedicated to Mary:

'The House of Mary' said to be the place where John took her to spend the remaining years of her life. Although the Roman Catholic Church has never pronounced the authenticity of the house it has become a place of pilgrimage and received visits and Apostolic Blessings from several popes including Pope Paul VI, Pope John Paul II and Pope Benedict XVI. Pilgrims are said to drink from a spring under the house which is believed to have healing properties and a liturgical ceremony is held every year on August 15th to commemorate the Assumption of Mary.

A further memorial to the Virgin the 'Byzantine Church of Mary' once served as the Cathedral of Ephesus, with the bishop in an adjacent palace throughout Late Antiquity.

The present structure is said to be the remodelling of a former stoa, which originally formed the southern edge of a large temple complex dedicated to the emperor Hadrian.

When John came to Ephesus, he not only became one of the leading founders of Christianity, but he also wrote his Gospel and last will during his stay. At his death he was buried on the side of the hill of Ayasuluk, to the north-east of Ephesus, within the fortifications of a Byzantine citadel. In the fourth century a small church was erected over his grave. In the sixth century the Emperor Justinian and his wife Theodora replaced the original church with a splendid basilica which became the centre of pilgrimage for almost 1,400 years until the Muslim invasion of Ephesus. Further destruction was caused by earth tremors. Today the original tomb of Saint John is believed to be located where the main altar of the basilica once stood. Covered by a large marble slab, topped by a Greek column, the grave is identified by an engraved stone marking its position.

Fr Mark celebrating mass by the Sea of Galilee

Statue of Christ standing over Peter

Fishermen casting beaded net

Shepherd's Field Church

Nativity Fresco

Dome of the Rock – Temple Mount

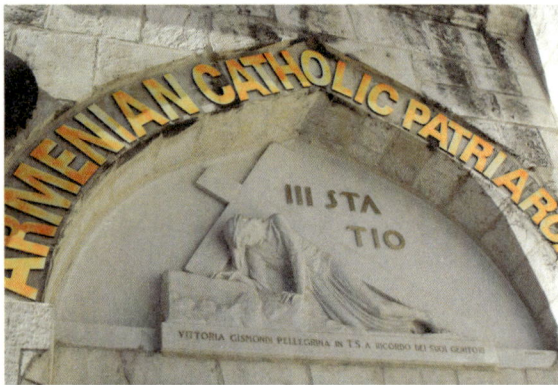

Via Dolorosa, Stations of the Cross

Hajia Maria & Church of the Holy Sepulchre

Aphrodite's Rock, Paphos

Tombs of the Kings, Paphos

Zoodochou Pigis Monastery, Samos

Stone Barn Church, Panagia

Angle of Annunciation Frescoe

Fresco Neophytos Cave

Saint HIlarion Castle

Remains of Bellapais Abbey

Saint Barnabas Monastery

Salamis, 4th century Christian Capital of Cyprus

Whirling Dervish

Attaturk – Father of Democracy

Limestone terraces – Pamukkale

Pirate ship

Site of the tomb of the Apostle Philip

Waterfall over Antalya Harbour

Medieval Caravanserai on the Silk Road

Caravanserai Dining Area

KAPADOKYA LODGE Cappadocia

Fresco hanging on lodge wall

Cave settlements & churches of Byzantine Chrstians

Rock Cut Christian settlement

Church of the Serpent fresco, Constantine the Great & the Empress Helena.

Odeon Theatre & meeting place

Monumental Gateway, winged angel of victory

Trajan Fountain, dedicated to Emperor Trajan

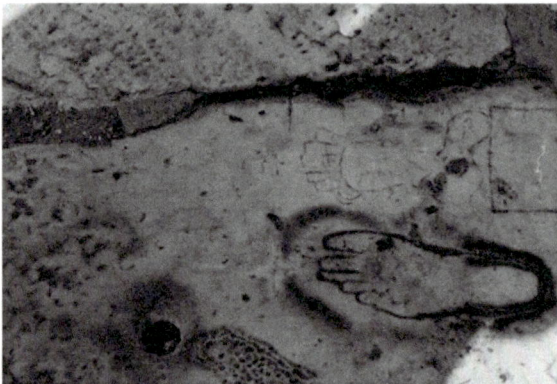

Footprint, pointing to brothel

Azure Window, Gozo Island. Collapsed in a storm that night, 8th March 2017

The Celcus Library

Acropolis of Lindos, Rhodes, portrait

Acropolis of Lindos, Rhodes, landscape

View of St Paul's Bay from Acropolis, Rhodes

Agios Georgios Church & bell tower, Lindos

Triton Fountain, Valletta

Statue of Queen Victoria, Republic Square

Saluting Battery, Upper Barraca Gardens

Monument, Sir Alexander Ball

Statue, Sir Winston Churchill

Monument to sailors who lost their lives in World War II

Saint Agatha statue, entrance to Crypt & Catacombs, Museum

Seige Bell Memorial

Basilica of Saint Peter

Michaelangelo's statue 'La Pieta'

Entrance to Saint Peter's Square

Statue of Saint Peter

Crowd waiting for Papal blessing in Saint Peter's Square

View to Basilca of Saint Francis of Assisi, from guest house

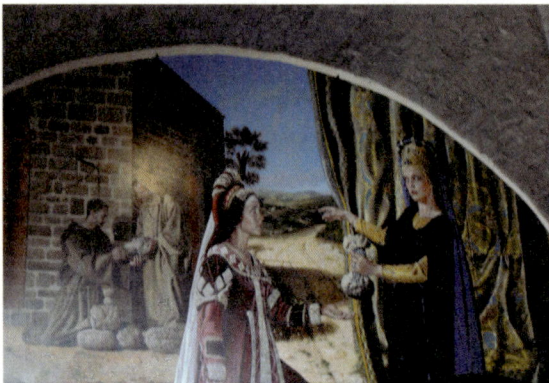

Image of Clare renouncing her wealthy lifesyle

Santa Maria Degli Angeli, Order of the Poor Clares

Statue of Saint Francis seated in the garden of the Poor Clares

Saint Francis holding a snake.

Celestial Cruise

Athens

The journey began with an early morning taxi ride to Gatwick Airport for a flight to Athens where a pre-arranged 'pick up' taxi took us to an overnight hotel. We arrived to discover that it was a bed and breakfast hotel – no food or drinks were on offer. As soon as we had keys to our rooms, we stowed our luggage, then set off along nearby streets to find a café or restaurant for an evening meal. The following morning another pre-arranged early morning lift took us to Piraeus Port to board the cruise ship.

Once on board our passports were taken, and credit cards registered. We then waited on the top deck until our rooms were prepared and we were given cards for access. Although we had booked rooms on the second floor with consecutive numbers, we discovered that they were nowhere near each other; we spent a good deal of time then and on the entire cruise getting lost in the maze of corridors. The rooms were quite narrow but comfortable: Two single beds separated by a small table at one end, a shower and wardrobe at the other end. Facilities included a small television with limited viewing and a telephone. The latter enabled us to keep in touch. Pre-warned about no tea making facilities we had packed our travel kettles. As soon as everyone was on board the ship set off for Kusadasi in Turkey, the port of call for the first excursion.

Ephesus

It didn't take long to discover that life on board was – and indeed with 1,664 passengers – had to be highly organised. Each day a slip of paper outlining the meeting place for excursions, the range of on-board activities, bars and restaurants was posted under the cabin doors – this plus information in English, then Greek was given over the P.A. system. There were ten decks. The top deck had a swimming pool, deck chairs for sunbathing and restaurants for pre-cooked meals or a buffet service. The buffet was especially useful to compensate for the limited amount of available gluten free food. Temperatures were pleasant but not high enough to tempt passengers to swim or sunbathe.

The first pre-arranged activity for everyone on board was the Lifeboat Drill. We were instructed to take the life jacket from the bottom of the wardrobe and follow signs to a specific area on the deck where a lifeboat was secured. We then followed instructions on how to put on and secure the jackets before boarding the boat. A 'Welcome Meeting' with the cruise director about life on board and shore excursions was next on the agenda. It was also an introduction to the huge number of passengers and the discovery that we were travelling in pre-arranged tour groups. The majority appeared to be retired American couples. Others were from Eastern Europe and Asia. As individual British passengers we were in the minority.

Ancient Ephesus throughout the Ages

After a 6 am breakfast on the following morning we made our way to Deck 5 – the meeting place for English speaking passengers to assemble and be organised into groups for excursions through Ephesus. There were three possible guided tours: 'House of the Virgin Mary and Ancient Ephesus', 'Ancient Ephesus and Terraced Houses' or 'Ancient Ephesus throughout the Ages'. Tour leaders for each group were holding flags. As individual travellers, we did not have the option of choice. 'Ancient Ephesus throughout the Ages' was on the cards. Then I saw a man holding a flag stating 'In the Steps of Saint Paul'. I made my way through the crowd to ask him if it was possible to join his group.

"Sorry," he replied. "It's pre-booked."

Although we wouldn't be able to visit the 'Grotto of Saint Paul' or the remains of the Byzantine Basilica built over his grave, nevertheless our tour did include those places connected with his ministry within the ancient city.

Once an important coastal trading centre, situated at the mouth of the River Caister Ephesus became dominant because of its strategic position and also because of its reputation as the guardian of the Goddess Artemis – one of the 'seven wonders' of the ancient world. At the time of Paul's visit (A.D. 52–54), it is believed to have been a place where people of all religions lived in comparative safety. Sadly, over the years Ephesus suffered a number of earthquakes and floods causing destruction of ancient sites and religious buildings. This, plus the silting up of the coastal port and harbour resulted in a dramatic decline in the population. It was when excavations and restoration of Greek and Roman remains took place during the mid-twentieth century that the ancient city became a highly visited site. A friend who visited in June said the number of tourists was so high that it was impossible to take 'people free' photographs of reconstructed, historic buildings. We were fortunate that tour numbers were comparatively low in late autumn.

We made our way to the parking area where a coach was waiting to take us to the Magnesia Gateway for the start of the tour along the Sacred Way – sacred because it was dedicated to the Greek deity Artemis – the twin sister of Apollo. Artemis was the goddess of the moon, the hunt, archery, the wilderness and fertility. Like all Greek Olympian Gods, she was believed to be immortal.

Although there was a distinct autumnal chill in the air, as we left the coach the sky was a lovely duck egg blue highlighting the remains of ancient buildings wedged between forested, mountain slopes. Our journey in the footsteps of our guide, who introduced himself as David took us to the scant remains of the former magnificent Temple of Artemis, where in 1956 a statue of the goddess was found. For years, the temple was a site visited by merchants, tourists, artisans and kings who paid homage to Artemis by sharing their profits with her. It also housed many artworks including sculptures, paintings and gilded columns.

When Paul first arrived in Ephesus, he met a number of disciples who were baptised in the name of John the Baptist. When Paul insisted that they should believe in the one who was to come after him – namely Jesus, they agreed to be baptised in the name of Lord Jesus. Since Paul's mother was a Jew and his father a Greek, he was able to preach in the synagogue and talk with Greeks in the pagan temples of Ephesus. Although, at the time of his visit there was a substantial Jewish Community – no traces of a synagogue have been found. Nevertheless, his preaching at the synagogue is recorded in Acts of the Apostles (19). Paul's ministry in the synagogue lasted for three months until the Jews began attacking him; he then held daily discussions in the lecture room funded by Tyrannus – a wealthy Ephesian. He is said to have preached here for a period of over two years.

We were now overlooking the remains of The State Agora: a large commercial marketplace. Surrounded by various colonnaded stoas and civic buildings it served as the city's administrative centre. The town hall contained the 'sacred fire' of the goddess of the hearth. Cult priests – known as Curetes were responsible for ensuring that the eternal flame, which symbolised the city's life, never went out. The Agora is also the place where Paul was able to earn his living by making and selling tents. (Acts 18). Paul learnt this profession from his father and grandfather – both were tent makers of the Royal Roman Army enabling them to receive Roman Citizenship and to pass the citizenship from father to son.

David was now making his way towards a row of stone archways that lead to the Varius Baths. First built during the Hellenistic era they were then enlarged during Roman and Byzantine Times and consisted of three sections: the *frigidarium*: The cold room, the *tepidarium*: the warm room and the *caldarium*: the hot room as well as latrines. The baths were situated near the main entrance to ancient cities so that visitors could be disinfected and wash before entering. In addition to the washrooms there were places for resting, sitting and reading. It is believed that ancient views about privacy were very different from those we hold today. The baths were also said to be places where early Christians socialised and conversed with fellow citizens. (Acts 18)

To one side of the baths were the remains of a large terrace on which was built the Temple of Domitian – dedicated to the Emperor Domitian (81–96 A.D.) who proclaimed himself as 'Lord and Saviour' as well as instigating the persecution of Christians. A seven-metre-high statue of the emperor is said to have been visible from every corner of the city.

The remains of the Odeon were next on the agenda. Built in the shape of a theatre it was also called The Little Theatre and served as a meeting place for members of the Senate as well as a place where social functions were held. A good part of the two levels of tiered seating were still in place. We continued towards the monumental gateway leading into Curetes Street: a downhill route towards the former harbour. Originally, the gateway had four sides linked by arches decorated with carved stele relief. Before us, the remaining Nike Relief – now balanced on a stone pedestal at ground level, represented the winged Angel of Victory. In her outstretched hand she holds a crown of olive leaves, also symbolising Victory. Then our attention was drawn to the marble slabs that still pave the street, reserved for horses and carts as well as Roman chariots. David explained that the marble was brought to the city from quarries, one of which was twenty kilometres away. The mosaic tiles which covered the sidewalks were still in remarkably good condition. I waited until the group had moved on before focusing my camera.

As we made our way towards the Trajan Fountain David gestured to the downhill view towards the Celsus Library, one of the most beautifully restored structures in Ephesus. He then explained that the original fountain, dedicated to the Emperor Trojan, who reigned between 97–117 A.D. was ornamented with statues of Dionysus and Aphrodite as well as members of the royal family. The statues are now exhibited in the museum.

Next our attention was drawn to the headless statue of a woman, standing in the remains of the *frigidarium* of the Scholastikia Baths: erected in honour of Scholastikia, a wealthy Christian woman who renovated the original baths in the fourth century A.D. In common with the Varius Baths they consisted of cold, warm and hot rooms as well as nearby latrines with a row of side-by-side seats, as well as a resting room, library and gymnasium. David then drew our attention to an inscribed footprint in a marble slab in the street that pointed towards the latrines. He explained that another word for latrines – found in an inscription in a nearby building, has been identified as brothel. The footprint was said to be an indication of the presence of both.

Situated close to the Baths the ornamented four columned portico of the façade of Hadrian's Temple rose before us. The original temple was dedicated to the emperor in honour of his visit in 128 A.D. Surmounted by a magnificent pediment the portico was decorated with classical motifs. At the centre the head of the Goddess of Fortune was still in place. Facing the temple were the roofed over remains of shops, where the well-off citizens did their shopping. At that time when Ephesus was linked by sea to all harbours of the Mediterranean, trade flourished. Behind the shops, on the lower slopes of the hillside homes of three storeys with central heating, plus an outside courtyard were built for wealthy inhabitants; workers and servants resided in the lower parts of the city in far less comfortable lodgings.

At last, we were standing before the magnificent, restored edifice of the two-storey façade of the Library of Celsus – built in 117 A.D. in memory of Celsius, the proconsul of the province of Asia. The façade is decorated with Corinthian columns behind which are three doors. In niches, between the doors are statues symbolising the virtues of Celsius: Wisdom, Fortune, Science and Virtue. The building served as a library where manuscripts and rolls of parchments were placed in niches. To protect the manuscripts from humidity, a passage was built in the masonry to permit air circulation.

Finally, The Grand Theatre – built on the slope of Mount Pion overlooking Harbour Street it was the first magnificent construction seen by travellers arriving by sea: The three levels of the reconstructed version take the breath away. This was a place where a Silversmith, called Demetrius provided work for a large number of craftsmen. As a result of Paul's success in converting people to Christianity Demetrius was no longer selling silver statues of the Goddess Artemis. Such was his anger that he stirred up a riot against Paul in the theatre. Fellow craftsmen started shouting, "Great is Artemis of the Ephesians." Paul wished to face the crowd, but the disciples wouldn't let him. The 'town clerk', who was responsible to the Romans for preventing riots then spoke up, reminding the people that since Paul and his followers were not guilty of any sacrilege or blasphemy against the goddess Artemis if they wanted to complain they must take the matter to court.

For Paul however, this commotion signalled that his time in Ephesus had come to an end. He sent for his disciples and, after speaking words of encouragement to them said goodbye and set out for Macedonia.

After completing his missionary journey Paul decided to avoid Ephesus and stop at Miletus on his way back to Jerusalem. From Miletus he sent for the Elders of the Church of Ephesus. His words to the Ephesian elders gathered at Miletus brought his time at Ephesus to a close.

'Now you see me on my way to Jerusalem in the captivity to the Spirit; I have no idea what will happen to me there…'

'Now I commend you to God and to the word of his grace…' (Acts 20:1)

When he had finished speaking, he knelt down with them all and prayed. By now they were all in tears; they put their arms round Paul's neck and kissed him; what saddened them most was his saying they would never see his face again. Then they escorted him to the ship.

From here they put out to sea and set on a straight course to Cos; the next day they reached Rhodes. (Acts 19–20)

Paul was not alone in being forced to flee from Ephesus. It was after the death and assumption of Mary that the disciple John travelled through Anatolia to spread the word of Christianity. He returned to Ephesus during the time of Domitian's persecution of Christians – he too was banished and fled to the island of Patmos where he lived between 81–91 A.D. It was here that he wrote the Book of Revelation addressing seven letters to the seven churches in Asia Minor. When the persecution ceased, he returned to his former home in Ephesus where he wrote his Gospel and Epistles. John is believed to have died in 100 A.D. at 'a great age'.

As we prepared to leave the theatre and make our way to Harbour Street David gestured towards the slopes of the forested hillside overlooking the silted-up harbour to the location of the 'Church of Mary'. He reminded us that the church has become a place of pilgrimage for visitors worldwide.

There was a surprise in store when we arrived at the coach. Before returning to the ship for the next part of the cruise we were visiting a carpet factory: a reminder that we were back in Turkey!

Finally, we were back on board and making use of the facilities before arriving at our next port of call on the Island of Rhodes. Our main focus was to follow in the steps of the Knights of Saint John – a powerful legacy to the missions of Saint Paul and his disciples. It was time to update on the history of the knights.

Their origin stretches back to the time when a group of monks known as the Knights Hospitallers established two hospitals in Jerusalem for the reception of pilgrims who became ill on their travels to the Holy Land: one for men and one for women. The hospital for men was named Hospital of Saint John Almoner, after a wealthy Cypriot who donated alms for the pilgrims. The monks then became known as 'The Hospitallers'. It was after the Crusaders captured Jerusalem that the knights took on a military role and became known as 'Knights of the Order of St John of Jerusalem'.

The Maltese Cross was officially adopted by the Order in 1126. Its eight points denote the eight obligations of the knights: To live in truth, have faith, repent one's sins, give proof of humility, love justice, be merciful, be sincere and whole-hearted, and to endure persecution. The members of the order consisted of representatives of seven exclusive major national groups: Province, Augergene, France, Italy, Germany, England and Spain. The latter were divided into Aragon and Castille, bringing the number of groups to eight. Each group had its own headquarters and place for lodging.

When Palestine was captured by Muslim forces in 1291, the Order moved briefly to Cyprus and then, in 1309 to Rhodes. The island of Rhodes – the next place on the agenda was also visited by Paul on his return journey to Jerusalem.

Rhodes

As we drew near to the island and headed towards the docking area for cruise ships, we passed *Agios Nikolaos* – Saint Nicolas Fort, guarding the entrance to Mandraki Harbour. The fort, along with two Italian crafted bronze deer, that replace the giant bronze statue of Colossus acted as a key defence to the city of Rhodes. The statue of Colossus – one of the seven wonders of the ancient world reached over three meters in height and is said to have taken twelve years to build (294–282 BC). Toppled by an earthquake (225–226 BC) the fallen statue was left in place until (664 CE) when Arabian forces raided Rhodes and had the statue broken up and sold for scrap. The fragments are believed to have totalled more than 900 camel loads.[3]

Once the ship was safely moored, we dismounted and followed directions to a coach that was ready and waiting to take us to Lindos where we would have the opportunity to climb the steps to the ancient citadel of the Acropolis. Its remarkable history includes successive fortification by the Greeks, Romans, Byzantines and the Knights of Saint John. In the 16th century, when the Turkish Sultan Suleiman the Magnificent conquered the island, the Knights were given safe passage and retreated to Malta. Over the years Rhodes suffered a great deal of damage. It was when the Italians took control in 1912 that important archaeological excavations and restoration took place.

Ear plugs in place we learnt that a number of films were made on this island including 'Guns of Navarone' starring Anthony Quinn. Apparently, Quinn so loved the island that he bought some land and had a house built. The driver also informed us that since the inhabitants needed time for harvesting the olives the island would shortly be closing to visitors. Once the coach was parked, we were met by a guide who directed us towards a pathway that took us to the start of the 250 steps leading to the Acropolis – originally built by the Knights of Saint John.

Set onto the side of the mountain the steps were high and steep, plus there was no supportive handrail. It didn't take long for me to realise that as a result

---

[3] *Editors: Encyclopaedia Britannica*

of ongoing joint problems the climb was not safe for me. Jill had stopped and was waiting alongside two donkeys that were tethered at the side of the steps. When, in desperation I asked her if she would be willing to join me and continue the ascent on one of the donkeys she agreed. Along with the owner Jill helped me onto the nearest donkey before mounting herself. Having long legs didn't help and within minutes I realised that it was an unsafe option and we both dismounted. While Jill was intent on setting off to catch up with the rest of the group, I explained that I would wait for her at the hillside restaurant we had passed and take the opportunity to do some more research from my *Glogetrotter Travel Guide*.

On my way down my attention was drawn to some women standing alongside the path selling handmade, lace tablecloths that were spread out on an outcrop of rock – a tradition that is said to go back to the time of Alexander the Great. Minutes later when I reached the entrance to the I, I discovered that it consisted of three levels – set into the side of the mountain. I made my way to the open-sided top section and was delighted to find splendid views down to the bell tower and rounded cupola of the church of *Agios Georgios* (Saint George). Embedded in the fortified walls of the medieval city, it is said to be the oldest of the island's churches. My photos were nothing to compare with those Jill had to show me when she arrived to join me for coffee. The massive, defensive walls of the Acropolis, the remains of the Palace of the Knights and a Byzantine church dedicated to Saint John were outshone by a splendid downhill view of the circular bay dedicated to Saint Paul – the place where tradition states that he is said to have landed and sheltered during a storm, in A.D. 51.

We arrived back at the coach to find the driver and a group of friends, seated in a circle at the foot of the steps leading into the coach, playing backgammon. Minutes later they were back on duty at various parked coaches, and we were on board and heading for the old walled town of Rhodes. Built alongside Commercial Harbour and surrounded by a moat on the inner side, the medieval walls and gates are a legacy to the Knights. Eight *Inns* of the Knights, one for each 'tongue' or nationality were built within the original Byzantine walls. Originally each section of the impregnable walls had its own gate but during Ottoman times two gates facing the harbour were blocked.

Our guided tour began through the massively fortified *d'Ambiose Gate*, built in 1512 by the Grand Master *Emery d'Amboise*.

As we entered, there before us was the imposing edifice of the 'Palace of the Grandmasters'. Restored in the 14th century the palace was used by the knights as a citadel within the city walls. From there a spacious walkway took us towards Saint George's Gate where our guide pointed to a bas-relief of Saint George killing the dragon, beneath the carved coat of arms of the Grand Master *Antoin Fluvion.* Our tour continued stopping at each of the gates where a relief or engraving made it possible to identify the home country of the *Inn.* On occasions I was able to photograph the top of historic buildings, visible through archways and over the gates – including the rose pink, domed roof of the Suleiman Mosque, built in 1523 to celebrate Suleiman's conquest of Rhodes. Our exit through Liberty Gate was a reminder that the Italians opened the gate in 1924 to celebrate liberation from Ottoman rule.

As we left the fortified city our attention was drawn to the Gate of Saint Paul, built in memory of his visit to the island while returning to Jerusalem from his third missionary journey.

'After we had torn ourselves away from them, we put out to sea and sailed straight to Cos. The next day we went to Rhodes and from there to Patara' Acts 21:1.

One tradition states that Paul's ship landed in a harbour at Lindos on Rhodes while another says that he travelled throughout the island spreading the gospel. Built in the second half of the 15th century the gate provided access to the fortified city as well as to Commercial Harbour. Surrounded by a low wall it was also fortified with two impressive towers to protect the city from the Ottomans. Severely damaged during World War 11 it was rebuilt in the 1950s.

While Jill set off on a further guided tour of the medieval city, I decided to take my time enjoying and capturing on film the Gate of Saint Paul as well as scenic views of the harbour before making my way back to the ship.

Santorini

Although the volcanic Island of Santorini was not on our list of places to visit, it would be an opportunity to take a cable car ride to see and capture on film some of the unique terrain including white-washed cubiform houses, clinging to the cliff-side as well as the village of Oia, perched on the Caldera

Rim. The volcanic history of the island is said to date back to 1650 BC when a massive eruption sunk the centre of the island, leaving a caldera, surrounded by towering cliffs. Further eruptions shaped the island as it is today. Evidence that the volcano continues to be active can be seen from steam venting from the nearby islet of Nea Kameni, within the flooded caldera, plus small tremors on Santorini itself.

By the time we were approaching the island it was late afternoon: the sun was setting, the sky clouding over, and a breeze was stirring up the waves. Since the loss of light plus unsettled weather meant that there would be few, if any photo opportunities both Jill and I decided to remain on board. Disembarkation by tender boats and access to the cable car by steep, rock cut steps were additional, possible hazards. We decided to retire to our cabins and meet up again in time for the evening meal. Sometime later I was awakened from a snooze by a loud clap of thunder, followed by lightning strikes visible through the cabin window and heralding the arrival of a storm – confirmation that our decision had been the right one.

It was when a couple, who had returned from the trip joined us for the evening meal that we learnt first-hand of the horrors experienced. When the storm was underway, everyone's priority was to return to the ship as soon as possible. It was on the discovery that the cable car had stopped operating that people started panicking and pushing against each on the steep, downhill steps, leading to the tender boats. A crisis point was reached when a lady slipped and fell. She was screaming loudly as nearby travellers tried and eventually succeeded in rescuing her. Although she had suffered a number of cuts and bruises, fortunately she did not appear to have broken any bones. It was an unexpected and dramatic end to the visit to the island of Santorini.

Crete

Finally, the island Crete where we hoped to have the opportunity to visit one of the two outstanding historic churches: the Church of Saint Titus or *Agios Minas* Cathedral. The establishment and spread of Christianity in Crete are closely associated with Titus – one of Paul's earliest converts. After his conversion Titus became a close personal friend of Paul's and a companion on his missionary journeys. Paul had visited Crete on his fourth missionary journey and was quite familiar with the island. When he returned to the island with Titus, he found that believers in the churches had no elders to serve as overseers or teachers. Paul and Titus set out to resolve the problem, travelling from city to city, establishing elders in each location.

Paul did not remain long enough to complete the process. After leaving he wrote a letter to Titus exhorting him to complete the task they had begun. It was a major undertaking for Titus especially as he is said to have faced a good deal of opposition. Nevertheless, he followed Paul's instructions and completed the mission, exactly as Paul directed. Finally, Paul appointed Titus as the first Bishop of Crete. The church dedicated to Saint Titus, first built in 1628 was reconstructed after World War 11.

Agios Minas Cathedral, dedicated to Saint Minas the patron saint of Heraklion was built in 1985. The saint's history in brief starts with his conversion to Christianity in adolescence. When he came of age, he decided to follow a career in the Roman army and served as a cavalry officer at the time of the ongoing Roman persecution of Christians. Roman soldiers were ordered to arrest and torture Christians to make them renounce their faith. Minas resigned from the army and decided to live as a hermit in the mountains. Tradition states that when he was about 50 years of age, a divine vision revealed that the time had come for him to suffer martyrdom. He then left the safety of his mountain home and returned to the city where he declared his faith. He was arrested, imprisoned, tortured and finally beheaded.

Once we had disembarked Jill and I decided to hire a taxi in preference to a sight-seeing coach tour. The owner, who introduced himself as George offered to drive us through the outskirts of Heraklion city and stop at a parking area close to *Agios Minas* Cathedral in order to give us time to explore. We were more than happy with his offer. Minutes later we were on our way and following a road close to Heraklion's fortified harbour walls – built by the Venetians. Meanwhile George was updating us on the more recent history of Crete starting with the German occupation. He explained that when the Germans occupied Crete there was a British plot to kidnap the German General and take him to Britain. A group of saboteurs, who knew the island well succeeded but with terrible reprisals from the Germans. The story, made into a film starring Dirk Bogarde, called 'Night Ambush' was filmed on Crete.

The sun was shining when we arrived. George pointed towards a road leading to the cathedral. Minutes later it was there before us. Its setting, above a series of steps and overlooking a wide *piazza* showed off to advantage the impressive cruciform style topped with a dome, as well as two bell towers. As we entered it took a while to adjust to the incredible frescoes and paintings covering the walls and domed ceiling – the artwork was assigned to Saint Kartaris who followed the principles of Byzantine icon painting. There were two aisles – one dedicated to Saint Titus and the other to the Ten Martyrs of Crete. Once again on my travels, it was the overhead painting of Christ Pantocrator that stayed with me.

As we left the building and made our way down the steps we came upon a statue of a Greek Archbishop. The inscription on the pillar, beneath the statue was in Greek so it wasn't until I did some research that I discovered that it was dedicated to Eugenios, a former Archbishop of Greece; a prominent Greek Orthodox Educator, he was also said to be a leading contributor to Modern Greek Enlightenment.

Back on board we discovered that disembarkation was at 7 am the following morning and our suitcases had to be packed and placed outside our cabins by 10 pm that evening. Since our flight to Gatwick from Athens was not until 8 pm it was going to be and, indeed was a long and drawn-out end to our memorable excursion with Celestyal Cruises.

Next on our agenda was to continue *On the Trail of Saint Paul* – this time on his final journey to Rome.

*****

In A.D. 57, when Paul arrived in Caesarea, after his third missionary journey he was held under arrest in Jerusalem for two years for preaching Christianity. Then in A.D. 59, under guard and accompanied by Luke and fellow prisoners he is put aboard a cargo ship to set sail for Rome where he is to be tried before Caesar. Paul had been shipwrecked on three previous occasions on his missionary journeys, but nothing can compare with the violence of the storm that he and his fellow travellers faced while crossing the Mediterranean en route to Rome. After fourteen days and nights the ship was finally wrecked off the coast of Malta. Our intention was to explore those places that are legacy to his three-month stay on the island.

Malta

Paul's Last Journey

We decided that March was a good time to visit Malta both for reasonable temperatures and before the fast-growing influx of package tours to this tiny pivotal island took hold. After some research we booked our flights and accommodation at the Hotel Kennedy Nova – conveniently positioned for ease of travel to places of historic and religious interest.

Across an inlet of deep blue sea, the outline of the dome of the Basilica of Our Lady of Mount Carmel crowned the hilltop of Valletta: Malta's tiny capital, built by the Knights of Saint John. Nearby, the spire of the Saint Paul's Anglican Cathedral tapered above a conglomeration of buildings towards the pale blue of the sky. I was standing on the balcony of my room, on the sixth floor of the hotel. Situated on The Strand, overlooking the waterfront of Marsamxett Harbour it was perfectly positioned both for the view and for travel. Sadly, it didn't take long to discover some of the downsides to this once upmarket residential area of Sliema.

For a start, an extremely busy road ran between the hotel and the beach. Added to this, men working on the scaffolding of a building in progress, attached to the outer wall of the hotel including that of my room, were busy hammering. To lessen the noise the balcony door had to be kept firmly closed. I left my unpacked bags and took a lift to the fifth floor to meet up with Jill. Even 'out of season' the nearby rooms we had requested some months previously were not available.

Since Malta was considered a safety zone, compared to Turkey, we were travelling independently and had decided to take a walk to see what expeditions were on offer for the following day from various booths scattered along the waterfront. Ongoing building projects between and behind high-rise hotels and blocks of flats that had replaced the original upmarket homes, made walking on the nearside pavements pretty hazardous. Our priority was to cross the road as quickly as possible. We navigated our way to the promenade along the waterfront; even 'out of season' it was busy with people advertising boat trips and historic tours.

Tempted by a half-day Harbour Cruise for the following morning with *Luzzu* (Fishermen) Cruises – the original local cruise company – we made our reservations. Luzzu, we learnt was now outnumbered and outsized by 'Captain Morgan Cruises'. Advertisements to *Join the Captain for a legendary party. Original Rum. Delicious cocktails* were not on our agenda. Furthermore, I had done some research and come across a number of downmarket reviews of Captain Morgan including:

'What a rip off – boat packed to the hilt – nowhere to sit down, except on the floor – food basic – cheap wine'. That was comparatively mild compared to a lengthy, highly critical report from a Canadian visitor that ended with: *'Never ever again!'*

Then, just as we were about to leave, we received and accepted a tempting offer: a day trip and jeep safari to Gozo Island, for the following day. After a quick wash and brush up at the hotel, we met at reception in time for the evening meal in the adjoining open-plan restaurant. Row upon row of neatly set tables, ready for an influx of visitors, stretched before us. We followed a handful of fellow early arrivals and set off to investigate what was on offer. Salads, soup, crusty bread and various sliced cheeses for starters, as well as a choice of meringue type desserts looked fine. On the other hand, the main course consisted of selections of meat and fish, steeped in thick unidentifiable sauces in large metal containers, plus two further containers one with a mix of overdone vegetables and the other squashed, roasted potatoes. Memories of warnings of lurking bacteria in food in similar containers in Turkey were revived but this hotel had no 'on-the-spot' cooked food as an alternative, so it was a matter of taking a chance or not.

While we were making up our minds a steady flow of visitors was moving in, including a large contingent of teenage boys. I ordered a glass of red wine from the bar and followed Jill who was helping herself to vegetable soup. I decided to do likewise, put safety first and restrict my menu to starters and desserts.

Harbour Cruise

A pink glow from the rising sun deepened and spread, lighting the harbour and cresting the silhouettes of a church dome and cathedral spire as we made our way to the waiting *Luzzu* cruise boat on the following morning. Seats on the top deck in lovely sun promised excellent viewing as well as photographic opportunities as we set off to explore the ten creeks of Marsamxett and the Grand Harbour that lay on either side of the heavily fortified peninsular, crowned by Valletta. As the boat headed towards the first creek alongside Manoel Island – now connected to the mainland by a bridge, a local guide with a hand-held microphone explained both its prime location and history as a hospital and fort.

In 1570 the island was acquired by the Cathedral Chapter of Mdina and became Bishop's Island – owned by the Bishop of Malta. Then in 1592, to cope with an outbreak of the bubonic plague a quarantine hospital was built on the island by the Knights of Saint John – at one time it is said to have held up to 1,000 patients. In 1940 it became the British Naval Hospital. We were interested to learn that huts constructed on the beach, were purpose built for use by the nurses who swam in the sea between shifts. The fort, to guard Marsamxett Harbour was constructed in the 1720s by the Portuguese Grand Master: Antonio Manoel de Vilhena – after whom it is named. Although, to this day Malta has not fully recovered from heavy bombing that took its toll on the island in World War 11, the commentator explained that plans are now underway to renovate the fort and create a marina for the ever-growing number of yachts crowding the two marinas at the neck of the inlet.

As the boat navigated downstream towards Fort Elmo – the formidable ramparts guarding Valletta – and into the open sea a brisk, cold wind greeted us. Built as a fortress city it was developed as a naval base by the British, who used part of the defences to moor and maintain submarines. Above us the towering, fortified eastern shore of Valletta is surmounted by *Sacra Infermeria* Holy Infirmary of the Knights of Saint John, as well as the Upper and Lower Baracca Gardens, built as a playground for the Italian Knights. Rounding the tip into the Grand Harbour we were heading towards and past the heavily fortified tips of two further peninsulas: Fort Saint Angelo and Senglea, the Knights previous headquarters. A great inland wall was built in the 1670s, as defence against the Turks attempted invasion. Then in 1565 the Knights strung a chain between the tips of the two forts to prevent the Turkish fleet of 200 vessels entering the harbour.

In the creek we were now approaching, the Knights developed a military naval base for their warships, which became known as Dockyard Creek. When Malta became a British protectorate in 1800 the Royal Navy inherited the facilities using it as a supply base during the first and second world wars. Today, the dockyards have been converted into The Grand Harbour Marina for the growing assortment of yachts. A number were moored mid-stream while both the shoreline and dry berthing areas were densely packed. Moorings for cruise liners, cargo and commercial vessels added to the growing congestion as we neared the end of the harbour where Malta Shipbuilding is stationed. As the boat turned to head upstream our attention was drawn to a large Swedish-built schooner: the 'Black Pearl' – reputed to have at one time belonged to Errol Flynn. Its colourful life includes being made to sink twice during the making of the film 'Popeye the Sailor Man', starring Robin Williams, in 1979. After being lifted, brought back on shore and restored, the upper deck was converted to house a fashionable restaurant while the lower deck is available to be hired for parties, receptions and discos, said to linger on till the early hours of the morning.

As we neared the tip of the Senglea Peninsula I made my way to the end of the deck. My intention was to capture, not only the stone *vedette* (watch tower) built on the tip of the bastion but sculpted images of an eye and an ear said to represent guardianship and vigilance. We had already noted painted or engraved pairs of eyes and ears on either side of the prow on small, traditional *Luzzu* fishing boats, anchored in the harbour fronting The Strand. Referred to as the 'Eye of Osiris, or the Ear of Horus' – the Phoenicians god of protection from evil – they were believed to protect the fishermen from any harm when they are at sea.

Once again cold wind greeted us as the boat rounded Fort Saint Elmo into the open sea before heading to Sliema Strand. Appetites wetted by the half-day Harbour Cruise, we decided to take advantage of the free afternoon and nearby bus facilities to make a primary visit to the deeply historic city of Valletta.

"We could start at the *Sacra Infermeria* (Holy Infirmary)," Jill suggested. 'The Malta Experience'. an audio visual account, covers 7,000 years of history. It's followed by a guided tour of the Knight's Hospital – now the 'Mediterranean Conference Centre'.

It was a splendid plan that would serve to underline and clarify some aspects of the complex history touched on during the harbour cruise. As soon as we were on firm ground, we set off to find a pavement café for a snack lunch, albeit under scaffolding then made our way to the nearest bus stop along the waterfront. Within minutes of boarding we arrived at Valletta Bus Terminus, close to the piazza, before the entrance to the city. We dismounted to be confronted by another scene of work in progress.

Before us, in the centre of the *piazza*, trees were being planted in preparation for the instalment of the Triton Fountain: three bronze figures of mythological Tritons – Greek gods of sea, holding up a platter. Inspired by the seventeenth-century Triton Fountain in Rome this modern version – originally designed and constructed between 1952 and 1959 deteriorated over subsequent years and was now in final stages of restoration. Further work in the *piazza* included the laying of stone slabs to form a wide, modern walkway over the dried-up moat leading to the city entrance. Apparently, there has been some ongoing controversy regarding the non-replacement of the former Italian designed ornate archway. Overall, the policy is said to make the square a safe place for pedestrians as well as to cater for the fast-developing tourist industry.

We later discovered that ongoing work throughout Malta was preparation for 2018 when Valletta will be a candidate for the 'European Capital of Culture'. Unsure of the route to our destination we decided it would be sensible to hire a traditional taxi rather than taking the more adventurous options of a drive-yourself, electric buggy or a lift in horse-drawn cart.

Safely delivered at the Infirmary we purchased tickets and made our way down to the purpose-built cinema in the basement. With a commentary by David Jacobi, the forty-five-minute account covered the turbulent history of the island from early settlers of the Temple Period to the Knights of the Great Siege through to the World War 2, preparing us for a tour of the former hospital and today's Conference Centre. The sheer size of the wards took the breath away, especially the 155m Long Ward. Overhead, the arched, arcaded ceiling was softly lit by candelabrum that had replaced the former candles. There were no windows, but ventilation was in place in the upper levels. Each patient had a bed, plus personal facilities including a lavatory, as well as a blanket in a colour that indicated the nature of his illness and treatment.

We learnt that the Knights were not only ahead in their knowledge of medical treatment but in anti-infection techniques, including the use of silver for medical instruments. After pointing to a ward for the dying with a small adjoining chapel, off the Long Ward our guide took us to the former central courtyard. Now roofed over, it is the Republic Hall, the main venue of the Conference Centre. Our tour ended with a visit to the State Dining Room, adorned with portraits of the Presidents of Malta and one of Queen Elizabeth as Queen of Malta. Between 1949 and 1951 the Queen – then Princess Elizabeth – lived on the outskirts of Valletta with her husband, Prince Philip who was serving as a naval officer; it is said to be the only place outside of the UK that she has ever called home.

It was after the war that the movement for self-determination grew stronger and finally Malta was granted Independence in 1964. That Malta was part of the British Empire for over 150 years is still evident in a number of ways: English is a joint official language with Maltese and to this day is fluently and widely spoken. Walking through Valletta one comes across shops and cafes with British names, red letter and phone boxes as well as driving on the left – all of which make one feel at home.

As we left the infirmary Jill decided that she had a good idea of where we were and of the way back to the bus station and set off down a cobbled street towards one of the harbours and then alongside of it. Believing she had a better sense of direction than I had I started to follow her but with some misgivings. Just as I called to her to stop and was about to ask a passer-by for directions a horse-drawn cart stopped alongside.

"Where are you going?" asked the driver.

When I told him we wanted the bus station, his immediate response was.

"Wrong way. Get on! I'll take you."

By now Jill had retraced her steps to join us. We negotiated a fare with the driver, climbed up and onto a cushioned seat. Within minutes I was mesmerised by the steady clip-clopping of hooves and the never-ending sense of history as we encountered and passed: narrow cobbled streets, boxed balconies, ornate baroque architecture, a huge square overlooked by a stately neo-classical building, fronted with Corinthian pillars; sculpted monuments and statues, red pillar and post boxes, church domes and spires. It was a memorable end to a tightly packed day.

Gozo Island

An early morning start for a doorstep minibus pick up to Cirkewwa Ferry Port, on the northern tip of Malta for a twenty-minute crossing to Gozo's Mgarr Harbour in preparation for a Jeep Safari. The route took us through steep, narrow, winding roads then headed through open countryside dotted with hillocks. A stiff, breeze greeted us as we boarded the ferry. Undeterred, Jill made her way to the outer walkway alongside the lower cabin while I opted for a sheltered, indoor window-seat. As we approached the former fortified harbour, historic landmarks were taking shape; with my camera securely strapped round my neck, I joined Jill and stood with my shoulder wedged against the railings to capture the remains of the former fortified harbour, two churches perched on the top of the hillside and the Gothic church of Our Lady of Lourdes – so-named because the rocks of the hillside were said to resemble the Grotto of *Massabielle Lourdes*, in France. I could just make out the statue of the virgin – carved by Antonio Busuttil it was placed in a natural cavity beneath the church. It is said that people from all over Gozo flock to the chapel to celebrate mass on February 11th, the date when Bernadette saw her first apparition.

By now, such was the increase in the strength of the wind that it was a challenge to remain upright and focus the camera, this time on the towering belfry of Ghajnsielem village church. I had been fascinated to learn that the name *Ghajnsielem* means 'a peaceful spring' and refers to a freshwater spring, around which in 1700, the Grandmaster Perillos built an arcade containing public washbasins.

Just minutes later the ferry lurched into the harbour and was secured to a mooring. It was a relief to disembark, be warmly greeted by our driver-cum guide and taken, along with a young couple to board his open-sided Range Rover. After introducing himself as a local man called Jake, he asked for our names. He had no problem with Adrienne, David and Jane but to our amusement, Jill was mistakenly referred to as Bill, then and throughout the trip.

First on the agenda was a visit to the Rotunda church of Saint John the Baptist. The outline of the huge central dome of the church, silhouetted against blue sky grew before us as we climbed the hill towards it. Jake was highlighting some of its history, he then stated that the miracle of the unexploded bomb that we knew from our research took place in Malta's Mosta Rotunda church, had taken place here. We exchanged glances but remained silent at this unexpected, false claim. Jake then went on to explain that the present church was built in the 1950s, round the remains of the original much smaller church, which has been rebuilt alongside and now serves as a Sculpture Museum.

From the moment we stepped inside the doorway the sense of space from the huge dome over our heads as well as light streaming through a circle of windows, highlighting the white limestone walls and columns supporting the dome, took the breath away. Polished marble floors and a selection of fine sculptures and paintings added to the ambience and sense of spirituality of this splendid church, dedicated to Saint John the Baptist.

Jake explained that there was a lift that could be taken from the Sculpture Museum to the top of the dome with splendid views across to Malta – because of increasing wind levels he advised against it. This was confirmed from the moment we stepped outside to board the jeep. As a result of an ongoing knee joint problem, I had been allocated the largely protected, front passenger seat while Jill and our travel companions were open to the full force of the elements on the seats at the back of the vehicle.

The route to the Citadel, our next port of call was along narrow streets lined with newly built houses. Similar in style and height to the original houses they were far more tasteful and less dramatic than current building projects in Malta.

Our first glimpse of the Citadel's fortified walls, crowning the hillside confirmed its defensive position and conjured its longstanding past. Believed to have been the centre of activity from Neolithic times, it was fortified during the Bronze Age, around 5,000 BC. In Roman times the Citadel was the centre of administrative, as well as military and religious life. The northern walls were built under the Aragonese, in the early 15th century while the southern side was reconstructed under the Knights of Saint John between 1599 and 1603.

The darkest period was the climax of Turkish attacks on Gozo in 1551. The medieval walls were overwhelmed and with the exception of some elderly citizens, the entire population was chained and taken into slavery. It took 50 years to re-populate the island and rebuild the Citadel. Although Malta too suffered from brutal Turkish attacks, its miraculous survival came in 1556 when reinforcements from Sicily arrived to help the Knights and the invaders fled – a victory that continues to be celebrated every year.

Safely delivered, we headed for the entrance archway to be greeted by the majestic sight of the Baroque façade of the Cathedral, dedicated to the

Assumption of the Virgin Mary (*Santa Maria*). The entrance doorway overlooked a flight of wide steps, guarded by two cannons before descending to a *piazza*. Jake gestured towards narrow streets leading from the square to various museums, as well as the Law Courts and the Bishop's Palace before taking us on a speedy, wind-swept walk along a section of the ramparts. We were rewarded by splendid views over Gozo's hills and valleys and across the sea to Malta.

"Come!" Jake called. "We'd better get to the coast before weather conditions worsen."

As soon as we were on board, he headed for Dwejra, a region on the west coast famous for its coastal rock formations, notably Fungus Rock and the Azure Window. As we neared the coastline Jake slowed down and gestured towards a chequerboard of rock-cut saltpans.

"Part of the centuries-old tradition of Gozitan Sea-Salt production," he explained. "Passed down in certain families for generations. During the summer months," he added. "Locals can be seen scraping up the crystals of salt. Once collected it is stored and processed in caves that have been carved into the coastal rock."

The distinctive outline of the saltpans, protruding into the sea remained alongside of us until we started to climb uphill towards a flat-topped headland. Parked within a few metres of the cliff-edge we were perfectly positioned to overlook the 60 metres high historic rock. Jake explained that it is a remnant, of what was once a sea cave – its roof had collapsed, isolating it from the sheer cliff face that it had once been attached to. Its fascinating history began when the Knights discovered a rare plant growing on the rock, whose red juice was treasured for its medicinal properties against dysentery, bleeding and impotence. It was used by the Knights to treat the wounds of sailors and soldiers. Such was its success that it became highly sought after – so much so that the sides of the rock were smoothed to remove footholds, plus a 24-hour guard and the threat of imprisonment for unofficial pickers. Later, it was discovered that it was not a fungus but a small parasitic tuber that feeds on salt tolerant plants – nevertheless, Fungus Rock still bears the original name of this world-famous product. Since its discovery by the Knights the plant has been found in a number of other Mediterranean locations as well as in Asia, the Canary Islands and Afghanistan.

Meanwhile, we were all busy attempting to ignore the wind and focus our cameras. While David and Jane were occupied taking selfie shots, I handed my camera to Jake, who had agreed to capture an image of Jill and myself with the 'world famous' rock in the background. That done it was a short ride to another sloping headland. This time our focus was a great arch of rock overlooking the luminous blue of the Inland Sea: the Azure Window. Once again, wind levels were high. Warned by Jake not to go any closer to the edge I had to be content with a photograph that captured the upper section of the archway. Fortunately, the Inland Sea was included. Today, the high demand option of a boat trip from the Inland Sea – once a large cave before its roof collapsed – through a tall narrow cave and out, along the cliffs to admire the Azure Window was not on offer. Given the weather conditions it was not surprising that we were the only visitors.

"The best view is from Dwejra Tower," Jake explained. "One of a number of coastal watchtowers built by the Knights as a lookout for enemies. From this one they could also keep an eye on Fungus Rock. Used as an observation post in World War 11. There are excellent views from the top but too much wind today. We'll stop at a sheltered café for lunch before heading for the Ggantija Temples." His suggestion was greeted with unanimous approval.

En route to the temples we were taken on a brief detour for an outside viewing of the Sanctuary of the Blessed Virgin *Ta' Pinu*. Positioned between two hills the basilica overlooked surrounding countryside. My Bradt Guide updated me on its history. Built between 1920 and 1931 on the site of a former chapel named after Pinu Gauci, who spent time and money repairing it in the 1670s; its history of 'spiritual' interventions created a sense of intrigue and wonder. The story told is that in 1575 a workman sent to demolish the original chapel suffered a broken arm when he struck the first blow. This was taken as a divine signal and the chapel was saved. Three centuries later two local people, who visited the chapel to pray for sick family members claimed to have heard the voice of Our Lady, who answered their prayers. Since then, the Sanctuary has become an important pilgrimage site – to this very day the number and range of heavenly interventions and miracles contribute to the spirituality and belief of the local people. Pope John Paul visited and said mass on the front terrace during his visit to Gozo in 1990.

I knew that the Sanctuary of *Ta' Pinu* was not alone in its claims of spiritual intervention on this small island. I had been fascinated to read an account of a remarkable miracle in the nearby tiny *San Dimitri* Chapel. Apparently, an altarpiece depicts Saint Demetrius riding a white horse – at his feet, a woman is praying and a man in chains. The legend told is that one night the village was attacked by Turkish invaders who carried off the woman's only son. The woman ran to the chapel to ask Saint Demetrius for help and promised to keep an oil lamp alight for him always. As she wept and prayed, the saint rode out of the picture on his white horse, gave chase to the Turkish invader and returned with her son in his arms.

Although the original chapel, in which the woman prayed fell into the sea when the cliff under it collapsed, sailors and fishermen are said to see the light still burning, below in the water. The present chapel, built in 1736 keeps a candle burning in its front hall beneath a copy of a poem about the legend.

Our journey continued from churches with legends of spiritual visions to a megalith temple complex, built in the Neolithic period (3,600–2,500 B.C.) Some of the megaliths are said to exceed five metres in length and weigh over fifty tons, giving credence to the belief that they were built by a giantess and named *Ggantija*: Giants' Tower. First excavated in 1827, two temples stand alongside each other surrounded by a boundary wall. Jake proudly reminded us that it was the oldest of Malta's extraordinary temples and a UNESCO World Heritage Site.

The Ggantija Temples, along with the remains of a number of other pre-historic sites are located in, or close to the village of Xaghra. It is believed that at one time there was an extensive Neolithic settlement with a stone circle, as well as underground burial sites and caves where the remains of Ggantija-phase pottery were discovered. En route to the temple Jake stopped alongside yet another Gozitan historic artefact: the 18th century Ta' Kola Windmill.

"Named after the last miller *Zeppu ta' Kola* (Joseph, the son of Nikola)," he explained.

"One of the few remaining that were built by the knights and leased to millers. When the wind was strong enough the miller sounded a large Triton-shell[4] to let the villagers know to bring their grain for milling." Before us, the cylindrical stone tower rose from a square base housing a number of rooms on two floors, including the workshop and living quarters of the miller. Although our entry tickets to the temple included a visit to the renovated rooms of the mill, complete with displays of traditional tools, furniture and items related to Gozitan crafts, time was not on our side.

Minutes later we were parked close to the temple. Collars up and jacket fronts pulled tight we followed Jake to the Interpretation Centre, the main entrance to

---

[4] *Tritons: Greek Sea Gods*

the site, where we had the opportunity to explore various aspects related to life in Neolithic times as well as to see a selection of prehistoric artefacts. Pointing to his watch Jake said he would meet us at the entrance in an hour.

The display included remains of animal bones found on the site, suggesting a ritual involving animal sacrifice as well as 'stick' figures and the remarkable 'Fat Ladies'. The 'stick' figures resembled carefully crafted pegs with the bottom end squared off – the right size and shape for holding in one's hand suggesting that they may have been carried in some kind of ritual.

The most intriguing were the 'Fat Ladies'. Typical of the temple period statuary, the rotund figurines have huge hips and behinds covered in pleated skirts, with short conical legs peeping out below. They are believed to have represented a deity or to have some kind of cult status.

Just as I was about to follow Jill, who was ignoring the onset of wind-driven rain and making her way towards a wooden walkway between the two temples, Jake appeared.

"Quick!" he said. "Call Bill! Quick. Storm on the way. Have to head for port before ferries stop."

Even the adverse conditions could not detract from the breath-taking sight of huge megaliths lining either side of the walkway before us. Then mind over matter, I caught up with Jill and we made our way to the jeep where our travel companions were waiting. Jake had let down plastic flaps to give the back seat passengers some protection as we headed for the harbour.

Relieved to find that a ferry was preparing to leave we joined a queue and made our way to inner window seats. Loudspeaker instructions to fasten safety belts and remain seated followed. Minutes later the ferry took off in great whooshing movements from side to side. Such was the effect of the oncoming storm that it brought to mind the shipwreck of Saint Paul. I said a prayer of thanks when we finally arrived and were safely moored.

On the bus back to the hotel a road-sign to Saint Paul's Bay – the place where Paul and fellow travellers swam from their wrecked ship to the safety of this island was a reminder that a visit to the bay and the offshore island, dedicated to him remained high on our agenda.

It was a relief to arrive on shore, find our 'pick up' minibus waiting and be transported to the hotel. After a hasty help-yourself evening meal, we retired for the night. Windows firmly closed I sank into a deep sleep. Jill was less fortunate. The noise level from a gathering of men in an adjoining room continued to grow until midnight when in desperation she banged on the door. It worked. Silence reigned.

Valletta

The following morning, we arrived at reception to be greeted by the startling news that the Azure Window had collapsed into the sea overnight. That we had been among the last visitors to see and photograph this world-renowned, natural rock feature took some absorbing. Although the sky had cleared, high winds persisted – boat trips and ferries had been cancelled. The relative safety of a bus into Valletta to visit some of the Knights' memorials to Saint John the Baptist as well as other historic places was on the cards.

As soon as we arrived at the bus terminus, street map in hand we made our way along Republic Street, the main route through the city to Great Siege Square. I stopped to photograph the impressive columned façade of the Law Courts as well as the Great Siege Monument: a granite base supporting three bronze figures, installed to commemorate the success of the 1565 Great Siege. A muscular male holding a sword which points down the centre of the monument, representing Valour is accompanied by two female figures dressed in flowing robes: the figure on the left representing Faith carries a papal tiara in her outstretched hand, while the figure on the right, carrying a mask of Minerva, represents Civilisation.

Finally, across the square the wide plain façade of the Saint John's Co-Cathedral, flanked by two bell towers was there, before us.

As we entered, we were given helpful, hand-held audio-guides. The interior, said to have once been as austere as the exterior underwent extensive transformation in the 17th century when Baroque fashion took hold. The barrel-vaulted ceiling decorated with a series of oil-on plaster paintings by the Calabrian artist Mattia Preti centres on eighteen episodes in the life of John the Baptist. Preti worked in both Italy and Malta. In 1660 he was appointed a Member of the Knights of Saint John. Every inch of the interior of the cathedral is covered with artwork, gold paint or marble. We made our way down the central nave, lined with side chapels – each representing a different *Langue* of the Order: Important noble families of Europe dedicated to protecting the Catholic faith. Each Order competed for superiority until St John's became what it remains until this day: The most opulent church ever to be imagined.

One of the most memorable features has to be the floor, which is paved with the ornate and multi-coloured, inlaid marble tombs of the Knights. Recurring symbolic images include a sickle-wielding skeleton, symbolising death and an angel of fame, blowing a trumpet. I have to admit that walking over the tombs made me feel uneasy.

Next on the agenda was the 'not to be missed' visit to the oratory to stand before the *piece de resistance:* Caravaggio's painting of the Beheading of Saint John the Baptist – his largest and only signed artwork: 'Fra Michelangelo' is scrawled across the Baptist's blood. It was a bleak reminder of the tragic life of this highly gifted young man. Born in the town of Caravaggio, the artist lost both of his parents while still in his teens. Described as a highly talented but hot-headed he killed a well-connected Roman in a duel, fled south and boarded a galley, belonging to the Knights, to Malta. Accepted as novice by the Knights, he painted both Saint Jerome and the Beheading of John the Baptist. Sadly, once again he became involved in a brawl. This time with a high-ranking Italian Knight and was imprisoned in Fort Saint Angelo. Somehow, he escaped and boarded a boat to Sicily before returning to Naples.

He is said to have died mysteriously while waiting and hoping for a pardon from the Pope. My mission was to find a way back to the tourist entrance to purchase post-cards of Caravaggio's work, requested by friends and family back home.

A pavement café to one side of Great Siege Square, with retractable plastic windows to shield us from the wind was convenient for a lunch break before a hasty visit to The Church of Saint Paul's Shipwreck. Once again, the simplicity of the outside belied the ornate interior – floor to ceiling covered with elaborate gilded frescoes and paintings, paid for by wealthy members of the Knights. Among the glitter, marble and gilt are frescoes from the life of Saint Paul and an elaborate altarpiece festooned with silver, while the dome is covered with Biblical scenes from the Maltese artist Lorenzo Gafa.

Whereas the overall feeling in Saint John's Co-Cathedral is one of celebration, the Church of Saint Paul's Shipwreck is both smaller and darker, even overcrowded. This, plus the discovery that it is the final resting place of two relics from the saint's tragic end – his wrist bone and part of the wooden column on which he was said to have been beheaded in Rome, left one feeling rather sombre.

Finally, the Manoel Theatre: commissioned by Grand Master Antonio Manoel in 1731 it remains one of the oldest theatres still in use in Europe. It was good to learn that, as well as looking after the sick and the poor the Knights were able to relax and enjoy 'honest entertainment'. Although its history does include a period when it was used as a hostel, the restoration as a theatre took place in 1960. Once again, we were given a hand-held guide, with ear plugs and commentary in a chosen language to accompany us through the museum and into the theatre.

As we entered and made our way to the stalls for the afternoon performance we were enveloped in a strong sense of the past: tiers of ornately decorated boxes, crowned by a gallery area, covered by a gilded ceiling restored from the time of the Knights. This plus the audio visual spectacular of 'The Malta Experience': 7000 years of history – from early settlers of the Temple Period to the Great Siege through to World War Two – brought to life events that have shaped this tiny island's dramatic history.

After a hassle-free bus journey back to the hotel we were in time for a light meal of 'starters' and 'desert', in the 'about to be opened' restaurant before retiring to our rooms. Delighted to find that the men, working on the building next door had retired early, I closed the balcony windows to lessen the noise of non-stop traffic and prepared for an early night. Within minutes I fell into a deep, undisturbed sleep.

Mdina

The Silent City

A visit to the medieval, walled city of Mdina was our priority on the following morning. After a number of failed attempts to arrange transport from the hotel – available only during the tourist season – we discovered that a local 'Hop On. Hop Off' bus service not only went to the ancient capital, but we could 'Hop Off' en route to visit the Miracle Church of Mosta.

In spite of persisting wind and the open top of the bus we opted for seats on the upper deck both for the views as well as photo opportunities. As we approached the church, I was able to capture an image of the huge miracle dome. Miracle because in 1942, as a congregation of around three hundred attended afternoon mass, a German bomb broke through the dome and thudded to the church floor but did not explode. No one was hurt or injured. Known as the Mosta Dome or the Rotunda it dominates the town and overlooks the surrounding countryside. It was time to 'Hop Off' the bus and stop at a nearby coffee shop before visiting the church.

As we entered the church the sense of space and coolness from the white, blue and gold of the inner surface of the dome was a reminder of Gozo's Church of John the Baptist – both laid claim to having the third largest unsupported dome in Europe. However, Jake's claim of an unexploded bomb in the church in Gozo went too far! In both churches the sense of space is reflected in the marble floor leading to side chapels dedicated to the Knights.

Mdina – was next on our itinerary of places to 'Hop Off'. Strategically placed on the edge of a plateau, overlooking the surrounding countryside it has been aptly described as 'lording it over all it surveys'.5

Its complex history in brief goes back to the Bronze Age and Roman domination until the 10th century when the Arabs took control, before giving way to the Normans. Under the Knights, in 1530 the town's defences were strengthened. However, at this time the Knights needed to be closer to their ships for defence purposes. They based themselves in Vittoriosa, then Valletta while Mdina became the seat of Maltese nobility before going into a period of decline. Extensive damage, caused by a severe earthquake added to the disrepair of churches and houses.

This was rectified in the early 18th century when the Grand Master, Vilhena commissioned major refurbishment. It was when the French arrived in 1798 and looted Mdina's churches that local people began the rebellion that eventually brought the brief rule of the French in Malta to an end and the British were ushered in.

The bus dropping off point was close to a flight of steps leading to the Main Gate through Mdina's heavily fortified walls into Saint Publius Square. Steeped in the history of Publius, the Roman Governor of Malta, it was an appropriate starting point. In fact, we discovered that the square was also dedicated to Saint Paul and Saint Agatha – the three patron saints of Mdina.

There, before us on the inner side of the Main Gate a sculptured relief portrayed Paul at the centre with Saint Publius, his first Maltese follower to one

---

5 *Bradt Travel Guide: Malta & Gozo, Juliet Rix*

side and Saint Agatha on the other. Saint Agatha became especially beloved by the people of Mdina when she succeeded in 'seeing off' a Turkish attack on the city. The tragic legend of her life began when, brought up by a noble family in Sicily she was asked to marry the Roman Governor, Quintianus. Insisting that she wanted to remain a virgin, married to God she fled to Malta in A.D. 249. The horrifying end to her life took place when she returned to Sicily in A.D. 251: she was imprisoned and had her left breast cut off before being stripped naked and burnt to death.

Our plan was to take our time exploring the labyrinth of narrow, cobbled streets leading to a network of squares dedicated to prominent figures and overlooked by religious buildings, as well as the palazzi – (grand houses) of wealthy knights. That the streets were deliberately kept narrow and angled to protect against invasion was very soon apparent – so narrow that there was just sufficient room for the occasional traditional horse and cart to pass by and hopefully, pick us up should we get lost! Our focus was to get a sense of the unique history of the place from exploring and photographing the outside of buildings as we made our way towards Bastion Square at the far end, from where we could overlook the surrounding countryside.

The overriding sense of Christianity was present in the number of sculptured, saintly figures adorning the walls of houses, as well as life-size statues, especially of the Virgin and child. Somehow, we did manage to find our way to a pavement café in Bastion Square before enjoying views over the city's heavily fortified walls that looked across vineyards to Mosta's miracle dome. The slim dome of Valletta's Basilica of Our Lady of Mount Carmel was just visible across the increasing urban sprawl. A satisfying end to another historic day before making our way back in time for the 'Hop On' bus to Sliema.

The Upper Barracca Gardens

Greeted by sun and a light wind, Jill set off for her early morning walk along The Strand to Tigne Point, the place where the Knights built their last defensive fort; meanwhile I focused on completing my notes and doing some further research on The Upper Barracca Gardens in Valletta. Located on the upper tier of Saint Peter and Paul Bastion, the gardens were originally built as a roofed playground for the Knights. Today, they are no longer roofed but a place for visitors to relax in the gardens and enjoy stunning views across the Grand

Harbour. The gardens also provide access to the Saluting Battery of guns as well as to the restored Lascaris War Rooms.

The route from the bus station to Valletta was straightforward and we arrived in plenty of time before the traditional noonday firing of the Saluting Battery. A lift took us to the Upper Gardens where we made our way between arcades that once supported the roof before separating: Jill to visit the War Rooms while I decided to explore the gardens as well as to enjoy stunning views across the harbour. We agreed to meet for lunch at the outside roof café.

From my research I knew that the gruesome history of the dark underground tunnels of the War Rooms began when they were built by the Knights, as living quarters for their galley slaves between 1636–57. Dug, deep into the rock 150 feet beneath Lascaris Bastion, they then became the subterranean headquarters of Britain's War HQ in Malta, from where the defence of the island against Axis aggression was waged especially during the bombardment of World War 11. Radar warnings were received from Sicily of imminent attack from Italian and German planes. In July 1943, the War Rooms were used by General Eisenhower and his supreme Commander: Admiral Cunningham, Field Marshall Montgomery and Marshall Tedder for Operation Husky: the successful Allied invasion of Sicily.

Leaving Jill to find her way down a dark, narrow stairway for a guided tour I set off between the arcades to explore the gardens, making occasional detours to identify and photograph some of the sculptured monuments – mostly of Maltese and military men. These included Churchill, Eisenhower, Montgomery, Lord Strickland, General Patten and the Battle of Trafalgar hero Sir Thomas Fremantle – all of whom who played vital roles in the defence of this tiny and strategically positioned island.

Suddenly and unexpectedly, I remembered that Malta was one of the overseas places where my older and sadly, late brother Kevin had been stationed during his time of serving in the army. It must have been before 1979, when the British military bases in Malta were closed. I wondered if he had enjoyed the gardens and taken part in midday firing of the cannons?

Originally, bronze cannons that fired stone cannon balls were part of Valletta's defence system. Today, the battery consists of eight renovated British cannons that are fired at midday. I found a place where I could look down on the battery of guns pointing towards the Grand Harbour, just in time for the salute. Across the harbour further views included the historic Three Cities of Senglea,

Vittoriosa and Cospicua, where the Knights first settled in 1530. The three cities became one when they were enclosed together as part of the Knights 17th century defence system. The view brought back memories of the Harbour Cruise when we looked across from Senglea Point to the fortified walls of Valletta and the Barracca Gardens: a reminder that the harbour and its natural creeks made Malta so attractive to those powers who wished to control the Mediterranean.

I arrived at the café just in time to meet up with Jill. After a snack lunch, followed by a failed attempt to locate the Lower Barracca Garden – which we later discovered were in fact positioned on the top of a nearby hill, not much lower than that of the Upper Gardens – we headed back to the bus terminal.

When we arrived at the hotel a surprise was in store. The men working on the building next door were now in the process of attaching scaffolding to the wall of my room. Such was the level of noise and vibrations that I went to reception and asked for a change of room. The only room available, away from the outer wall was on the first floor. There was no alternative. The loss of views, across the harbour and an increase in noise level from traffic on the street below were preferable to the horror encountered in my vacated room.

Ghar Dalam Caves and Ancient Temples

On our final day we booked a coach trip to Ghar Dalam Caves and the ancient temples of Mnajdra and Hagar Qim. Along with Gozo's Ggantija Temples and remains of Neolithic settlements the temples were built nearly a millennium before the Egyptian pyramids and 500 years before the stone circle at Stonehenge. Ghar Dalam, meaning 'Cave of Darkness' was one of the first places to be inhabited by man in Malta. It is believed that descendants of Neolithic people built the nearby temple complex.

The coach parked on the doorstep of a museum, close to the entrance to the temples where the remains of dwarfed and gigantic prehistoric animals, discovered from the Pleistocene Era were on display. These included: hippo bones and prehistoric elephant molars, plus the slightly more recent and almost complete skeleton of a deer. It was during the Pleistocene era that animals travelled south from Europe to Sicily and Malta – then linked by a land bridge. It was when sea levels rose that the islands were cut off and larger creatures, including elephant, deer and hippopotamus evolved into much smaller species than their relatives in Europe: whereas the smaller species, including tortoise and dormouse became larger.

As we left the museum a long flight of shallow steps led to the cave entrance and into a long tunnel, formed by water percolating through the rocks. A walkway took us past still forming stalactites and excavation pits while a mound and pillar showed the various excavated layers and what was found in them.

The idyllic location of the Temples of Mnajdra and Hagar Qim on a south facing slope, where the coastline dips down to the sea ensured areas favourable for farming and provided easy access for boats to land nearby. These benefits were apparent from the moment we arrived: there before us, against a backdrop of blue sea and overlooking the island of Filfla – used for target practice during the World War 11, stood an open fronted complex of huge stones. Added to this the walkway to the site was lined with an abundance of scented, wildflowers.

Protective canopies, erected over the roofless site could not detract from the amount of thought, care and labour that must have taken place to create this prehistoric complex of three adjoining temples. The traditional oval forecourt leading to a passage between great pillars of rock, topped with equally heavy slabs – some weighing over twenty tons, raised the still unanswered question of exactly how they were moved and erected. Speculation includes: the stone was already cracked along fault lines, using the blocks they were then transported by rolling them along on spherical stones like those found outside the temples. Finally, it was presumed that a combination of sledges, rollers, ramps and levers were used, plus a great deal of man and animal power.

Of the three adjoining temples of Mnajdra, the South Temple is aligned to the sun at sunrise. We entered through a narrow passage lined with great pillars of rock through which the sunlight beams into an oval forecourt on the equinoxes. The forecourts are believed to have been used as a communal gathering place as well as for ritual activity: equipment for animal sacrifice, holes into which liquid offerings to the underworld might have been poured were discovered as well as statuary, including the 'Fat Lady' and other stone phalluses – we had first seen in the Ggantija Temples in Gozo – that suggested some sort of cult status, possibly a fertility cult. A porthole doorway, marked with pitted decoration looked into an apse with pedestal altars. Further along, through another porthole we could see a large central pedestal altar marked with tally holes related to the appearance of constellations of certain stars.

While I decided to spend more time exploring the Mnajdra complex Jill set off along a 500m path, lined with wild fennel to Hagar Qim. As its title 'Standing Stones' suggests it is outstanding for the sheer size of the stones as well as for its less sheltered position on an acropolis overlooking the sea. Both temple complexes are thought to be expressions of fertility – worshipping religion.

Our earlier than expected return to the hotel, plus a drop in wind level and increase in warmth from the sun led to a plan to go for a swim in the hotel's rooftop pool. This was thwarted when we discovered that the pool was not in operation until the tourist season was in full swing. We set off to walk along the coastline to find the best place to go for afternoon 'tea and cake'. Once again, it was a stallholder who came to our rescue. We followed the advice given to make for the top floor of the nearby Marks and Spencer. Not only were there lovely views across the harbour but it was the first cup of tea that tasted like English tea. This plus a slice of Victoria sponge cake for Jill – a further memorial to Queen Victoria: the queen is said to have regularly eaten a slice of the sponge cake with her afternoon tea – and a slice of lemon drizzle cake for me made it the perfect place to reminisce on the historic places we had visited as well as to discuss those footsteps and shadows that we did not have the time to follow. We made a resolution to return to Malta.

Afterword

Shortly, after our return to the UK we were shocked to hear the news of the murder of Daphne Caruana Galizia, Malta's best-known investigative journalist. According to a Reuters report the journalist was killed when a powerful bomb blew up her car. Caruana, aged 53 ran a popular blog in which she relentlessly highlighted cases of alleged high-level corruption, targeting politicians from across party lines. It is said that she had just left her house and was on a road near the village of Bidnija in Northern Malta when a bomb detonated and sent her car flying into an adjacent field.

The Maltese Prime Minister, Joseph Muscat, who faced accusations of wrongdoing by Caruana Galizia earlier this year, denounced her killing, calling it a 'barbaric attack on press freedom'. He announced that the U.S. Federal Investigation had agreed to help police investigate the killing and were flying experts to the island as soon as possible. Joseph Muscat said that he would not rest until justice is done.

It was a stern reminder that in today's changing world, no matter how friendly and welcoming people from other countries are – Malta is high on the list – nowhere is free from wrong-doing or unexpected and devastating events. The shocking news did not deter us from our plan to return to continue our journey in Malta, *On the Trail of Saint Paul*.

Return to Malta

After a recovery period of two years, following joint surgery it was time for the long-awaited opportunity to continue our travels in Malta. Jill arranged a 3.30 am taxi pick-up and we were on our way to Bournemouth Airport for the flight. We arrived to find the driver of the pre-arranged lift waiting to deliver us to the 'Preluna Hotel and Spa' – recommended by well-travelled friends – on the waterfront at Sliema. A further downside to the early morning start and arrival was the discovery that we had to wait several hours for our pre-booked rooms to be vacated and then prepared before we were given access. This put an end to our plan for an afternoon visit to Valletta.

When we were finally given the 'thumbs up' for access we were delighted to discover that the hotel more than lived up to our expectations. In addition to air-conditioning, tea and coffee making facilities, satellite TV, free Wi-Fi and a bathroom with a shower the well-insulated rooms had glass doors that opened onto large, sheltered balconies with outstanding views across the Mediterranean Sea but without the sight or sound of traffic.

The sense of satisfaction was completed when we met for the evening meal at the Triton dining-room, so named because of the splendid, uninterrupted views across the Mediterranean Sea needed by the Greek gods of the sea. Lovely classical music filled the air as we made our way past selections of fresh and 'on the spot' cooked food to a table positioned alongside the windows. As sunlight faded and bats streaked across the star sprinkled sky, we raised our glasses to celebrate our return to this historic island.

*****

Unexpected wind and rain greeted us the following morning. The most practical option was to travel by bus to Valletta and head for the National Museum of Archaeology. A former home of the knights, the museum now houses displays of original artifacts taken from Malta and Gozo's Neolithic and Phoenician sites, for their safety and preservation. Collars up we crossed the road to join a gathering of people at the nearby bus stop. As the numbers increased memories from our previous visit that the British tradition of queuing was not practiced in Malta were confirmed. Nevertheless, once on board we did both manage to find a seat.

A commendable Maltese tradition that is practiced is that those seats, lining either side at the front of the bus are priority for the elderly and disabled. This was confirmed when an elderly lady with a walking aid got on and was immediately offered a seat vacated by a young man. Roads in Malta are full of humps and bumps so standing can be a test of one's agility.

On arrival at the bus terminus our priority was to photograph the restored Triton Fountain, situated in the centre of a wide *piazza* close to the entrance to Valletta. A sudden break in cloud greeted us as we make our way towards the fountain. The main structure consisting of the three Tritons: Greek messengers of the sea with upper bodies of humans and lower of fish, holding a large seashell over their heads was there before us. The surrounding space as well as the sense of movement of the life-size Tritons revived the legend of the Tritons ability to control the waves of the sea in order to protect the island from invaders. Restoration was completed in time for the official inauguration, by the Prime Minister, Joseph Muscat a week ahead of Valletta's taking up its position as European Capital of Culture in 2018.

Once we had completed our photo shoot, we made our way towards and through the great bastion defensive walls into Republic Street. We arrived to find that the museum was currently undergoing further work on the Punic, Roman, Byzantine and Medieval Periods. Fortunately, artifacts taken from Neolithic sites that we had visited on previous trips were on display on the ground floor.

The exhibition began with a range of artifacts from the time when the first settlers lived in caves. These included changes in the style and size of pottery as well as some human and animal figures. Megaliths from the stone temples (3600 BC–2500 BC) decorated with various carvings with the use of primitive tools made from bone, stone and wood brought back memories of our visit to Hajar Qim, including a highly decorated altar; further displays included a stone slab carved with low relief fish from Bugibba as well as friezes of animals from the Tarxien Temples. Several of the monumental blocks were decorated with a variety of spirals and geometric patterns. A room, to one side the artifacts cantered on human representation. Among these were examples of Malta's 'Fat Ladies' – deities of a fertility cult that we had seen previously in the Ggantija and Hajar Qim Temples. Nearby there was also a clay model of the 'Sleeping lady' – lying on her side on a couch as well as a headless statue of 'Venus' of Malta and a selection of carved stone jewellery.

Since time was on our side, we decided to take the opportunity to visit the suburb of Floriana – on the far side of the square. Our priority was the church dedicated to Saint Publius – the former governor of Malta who was converted to Christianity by Saint Paul. In 112 A.D. Publius was martyred by Roman authorities, during the persecution of Christians and later became a patron saint of Malta. The building of the church dedicated to him started in 1733 and took 33 years to complete. After suffering substantial damage during World War 11 the entire edifice was rebuilt.

Although today, Floriana is a pleasant suburb of Valletta its history goes back to 1634 when fearing an attack from the Ottoman Turks, the Grand Master Antoine de Paule appealed to the Pope for help to strengthen Malta's defences. The Pope sent the Italian military engineer Pietro Paolo Floriani, to design and oversee the construction of the Floriana Lines: an outer defensive system of the capital city. The lines and later the city were named after him.

Originally planned in 1724 under the rule of Grand Master de Vilhena, the area was composed of two parallel streets that ran from the Triton Fountain to the defensive walls. The Gardens between the streets were made as a place for the young knights to exercise while the church, dedicated to Saint Publius overlooks a square that runs almost the full length of the gardens. Another feature of the square are the large conical stones that covered the granaries: deep holes dug into the ground where the knights stored their grains. Further developments include the Botanical Gardens containing various memorials to the knights, the circular compact Saria Church, built in 1767 and the Wignacourt Water Tower: Constructed under Grandmaster Wignacourt as part of an aqueduct system it was built to supply Valletta with water from the hills around Mdina.

As soon as we arrived at the church was there before us; its impressive size and exquisite design included a neoclassical portico, topped by a triangular pediment, flanked by a bell tower on either side with a statue of Christ the King standing on the apex of the façade: another photo opportunity not to be missed. Unfortunately, the church was not open, so we were unable to see the statues of

Saint Publius and Mary as well as the artwork, carving, gilding and marble of the interior. We had to be content with photographs of the outside.

We had some difficulty finding the right place for the bus back to the hotel in the overcrowded bus location area. Nevertheless, when we succeeded in locating the right stop and the bus did finally arrive, we were both able to find a seat. It was a relief to arrive on the doorstep of the hotel and return to our rooms to recover before making our way to the dining room.

Our plan for the following day was to visit the coastal region where Saint Paul was shipwrecked and take a boat ride out to the island where a statue of him has been placed. Although the rain had stopped and the sky cleared, wind that had swept most of the cloud cover away was now stirring up the waves on the sea. The prospect of possible shipwreck did not appeal so a change of plan – another visit to Valletta was on the cards. After some research we decided on the Grand Masters' Palace in order to see a selection of armour and weapons used by the Knights to safeguard themselves against invasion.

The Grand Masters' Palace

Built between 1573 and 1578 by the Maltese architect Girolamo Cassar, in the renaissance style the Palace served as the Grandmaster's residence for more than 200 years. Used by the French until 1800 it then became the official residence of the British governors. The Palace is now the Presidential Office and Malta's Parliament. It was after the Second World War that the collection of armour and weapons, held in Malta's War Museum was transferred to its present location in the original Palace stables, on the ground floor. We decided to take the bus into Sliema and follow the now familiar route along Republic Street to Saint Georges' Square, one side of which is taken up by the Grandmaster's Palace.

When we arrived, we followed directions to the entrance in Old Theatre Street, through a courtyard leading to the museum shop and office to purchase tickets as well as audio guides to plug into our ears. Instructed to make our way to the lower courtyard we came face to face with a bronze statue of Neptune, then another short flight of stairs took us into a corridor leading to the museum. The Armoury Collection included a large variety of items dating from the 15th century when the Knights still occupied Rhodes, covering some three hundred years of development until the Order left Malta in the late 18th century, as well as a section dedicated to the Great Siege. The display included not only arms of the common soldiers but also the enriched personal armour and prestigious weapons of the nobility as well as a large number of helmets. One example is that of a black suit embossed with gold made for the Grand Master de Wignacourt (1601–22) as well as a 16th century cuirass, engraved to look like a buttoned waistcoat. Examples of armour worn by the Orders' militia men included black plates and breastplates. Leather or quilted jackets were worn underneath for comfort. A further section was dedicated to armour worn during the Great Siege.

The display of weapons started with a variety of edged weapons, polearms and crossbows and continued with one of the largest collections of the worlds' firearms as well as 17th century swords, pistols, crossbows and muskets. Weapons used during the Great Siege included numerous examples of Oriental weapons including firearms and Ottoman sabers. Finally, the artillery section exhibit included thin guns that could be poked through defensive walls, a flintlock rocket launcher as well as examples of both large and small bronze cannons and mortars.

We left the museum heads buzzing with the splendid collections and their historic connection with the Sovereign Hospitaller, Military Order of Saint John. In spite of continuing wind and some light rain we decided to make for one of the street cafes lining the sides of Republic Square for a snack lunch before heading back to the hotel. It was also an opportunity to take a photograph of the marble statue of Queen Victoria; situated in front of the Bibliotheca (National Library), the statue overlooks the square. Constructed by the Sicilian sculptor Giuseppe, the monument was erected in 1891 to commemorate the 50th anniversary of her reign.

One of the most interesting features is the lace shawl that drapes over the queen's lap reflecting her love for the fabric. This was confirmed when the Queen sent a piece of the intricate fabric to London to be displayed at the 'Exhibition of Industries' in 1881. At the time of the Knights of Saint John, ornamental lace was introduced as a fashion accessory, to embellish the clothing of nobles and aristocracy. The Maltese cross was added to make it uniquely Maltese. At one point, lace became so sort after that copies of the most popular designs were made and sent to China for mass production. The craft of lace making – still practiced by women in Malta and Gozo – is said to go back to pre-historic times. Such was the impact of her visit that in honour of the Queen's

Diamond Jubilee in 1897 Rabat, the capital of Gozo was renamed Victoria and a defensive wall, between two forts – spanning the entire width of the island – officially inaugurated in 1897 was named the Victoria Lines. Various pubs and bars are also named after her.

Back at the hotel, just minutes after we had settled ourselves at our favourite table in the dining room, we were surprised by a sudden increase in noise level from excited voices from what appeared to be an overseas' tour group that were flooding into the restaurant: the females dressed in colourful, long flowing garments and wearing dangling, glittering, jewellery as if attending some royal occasion outshone the more soberly clad men. Fortunately, as they sorted themselves at various tables and began to select food to start the evening meal the noise level dropped, and we could enjoy the magical notes of Mozart's piano concerto as well as the scenic views across the wide expanse of the Mediterranean Sea.

Saint Paul's Bay

Although the weather conditions had not improved, in the hope that we would be able to locate a boat owner willing to take us out to Saint Paul's Island we decided to go ahead and risk a visit to Saint Paul's Bay. Dressed in the most weatherproof garments we had with us, we made our way to the nearest stopping place for a bus to Bugibba. This former up-market, coastal region for homes for the wealthy is now reputed to be a popular tourist resort containing numerous hotels, restaurants, night clubs, pubs and a casino.

Once again, the bus was overcrowded and the road chaotic and busy as it followed a route winding up and down hillsides, where spiny fingers of rock crossed infertile rock-strewn fields; some contained the remains of ancient buildings, various types of cactus and bony trees. Finally, the sea was in sight and before long the coach stopped at the Saint Paul's Bay end of Bugibba. Recovery was made by a visit to a nearby café where we ordered coffee and a toasted bacon sandwich. Despite the unfavourable weather we then succeeded in locating the owner of 'Sea Horse Cruises' – a small boat on the waterfront – who was willing to take us to the island. In order to make the trip financially worthwhile, he was hoping to attract further passengers. He looked at his watch and asked us to ready to board in half an hour.

It was an opportunity to locate and visit the nearby Church of Saint Paul's Bonfire. Built on what was traditionally regarded as the place where the fire was lit to warm Saint Paul, Saint Luke and their companions after they were shipwrecked in A.D. 60. It is also the place where Saint Paul is reputed to have bitten by a poisonous snake while collecting wood for a bonfire but miraculously showed no ill effects. Apparently, a bonfire is lit outside the church every year to celebrate the event. We set off towards the Saint Paul's Bay end of Bugibba. Once a traditional fishing village but now merged with Bugibba, it is the place where the original church, built by the Grand Master Wignacourt stood. Hit by a bomb in 1943 the church was reconstructed in 1957.

Although, now surrounded by modern buildings, the comparatively small church stands out for its position at the top of a flight of steps, overlooking the waterfront as well the simplicity of its design and structure: the apex of the facade supports a single bell which is topped by a cross. At the front of the building the central and tallest of three archways took us to the entrance door. Unfortunately, it was locked so we were unable to see the artwork of the highly decorated interior as well as a statue of Saint Paul that is still carried through the streets of Valletta on 10th of February to commemorate the day he was shipwrecked. Further treasures are said to include a relic of Paul's wrist bone and part of the pillar on which he was beheaded in Rome.

By the time we returned to the boat, although only three passengers were on board – a young couple and a single man – the owner, who now introduced himself as Peter was preparing to take off. It didn't take long to realise the advantage of having just three companions: we could change position for the best photo opportunities as well as to avoid the full force of persisting wind. As Peter guided the boat across the bay it rose and fell across windswept waves; Peter pointed inland towards the upper portion of a defence tower. Built by Grand Master Alof de Wignacourt, it is the oldest, surviving defence tower in Malta – now surrounded by a cluster of modern housing.

As we progressed the coastline became rocky and higher with open cavities worn by the waves. Peter turned the boat between two pinnacles of rock into a series of caves that magnified the sound of water threshing against the walls was a potent reminder of the storm swept sea at the time of the shipwreck. Before long we were approaching the island and could just make out the outline of the statue of Saint Paul crowning the hilltop.

Once the boat was safely tied to a mooring, alongside a platform of rock Peter helped us onto dry land and pointed to a narrow, stony footpath that led to the foot of the statue. While the couple opted to remain on the lower slopes I set off towards the summit with Jill and Andrew – a fellow passenger. It was obvious that Andrew was a keen photographer; like me he was armed with a Nikon camera and his priority was visiting and photographing historic places. While my super fit companions were intent on reaching the foot of the statue. I decided to take my time and attempt to find a position lower down, from where I could take a photograph.

Mission accomplished I made way to the boat. As soon as we were all on board Peter started the engine and we headed back. Thanks to his skilful navigating between and over threshing waves we avoided being shipwrecked and arrived safely onshore. Once again, the long and tiring bus journey back to Sliema was made bearable by the knowledge that we had the amenities and comfort of the hotel to look forward to.

Upper and Lower Barracca Gardens

On the following morning since strong winds and rough sea had not subsided – further travels by boat or ferry were not an option. We decided to visit both the Upper and Lower Barracca Gardens in Valletta. As soon as we arrived on the doorstep of Valletta we made our way along, the now familiar route through the bastion walls, into and along Republic Street.

In order to avoid the possibility of getting lost we decided to take a taxi to the Upper Gardens. Upon arrival, while Jill was keen to make a second visit to the World War 11 War Rooms, I decided to take the opportunity to capture on film the sense of history from various memorials in the garden as well of the fortifications of the island. We agreed to meet in time for the noonday firing of the cannons before enjoying refreshments at the restaurant followed by a pony and cart ride to the Lower Gardens.

Once again, the sound of hooves clip-clopping along, narrow cobbled streets revived the sense of the past of this historic city. We stopped just before the entrance to the gardens – a perfect position to photograph the Siege Bell Memorial. Positioned to overlook the Grand Harbour, the Siege Bell honours the 7,000 service personnel and civilians who died during the 1940–1943 'Siege of Malta'. A neoclassical cupola, containing a 12-ton bell tolls daily at noon. This memorial was unveiled by Queen Elizabeth 11 in 1992 – the 50th anniversary of the award of the George Cross, by her father to the people of Malta. Between the bell and the water, a bronze statue of a sailor being prepared for burial at sea remains as a sombre memorial to those World War 11 sailors who lost their lives defending the island.

By the time we entered the gardens several tour groups had already arrived. While Jill made her way to the war rooms my focus was to get some 'people free' shots of the incredible fortified walls and promontories guarding Valletta as well a fishing boat trailing a huge net across the harbour. Next my sights were set on a monument dedicated Sir Alexander Ball the British captain, later admiral who was instrumental in taking Malta from the French in 1800. Built in the style of an ancient Greek Temple the monument contains four statues representing War, Prudence, Justice and Immortality. Set amongst trees, overlooking a fountain and against a background of blue sky it was perfectly positioned.

Finally, a memorial statue of Sir Winston Churchill was a reminder of the part he played in Operation Pedestal: an operation to carry supplies to the island as it edged inevitably towards starvation and surrender in the summer of 1942. At that time Churchill was in Washington, where the chiefs-of-staff cabled him, urging him to request a loan of the tanker SS Ohio to deliver essential supplies[6] to Malta.. It was Churchill's friendship and collaboration with the film producer Alexander Korba that helped bring America into the Second World War. Churchill requested SS Ohio, plus two other warships.

The remaining merchant ships were British – all armed with anti-aircraft guns. A large escorting force was assembled to protect the convoy.

Targets achieved I made my way to meet up with Jill for 'tea and cake': a pleasant and satisfying end to our final visit to Valletta.

Rabat and Mdina

Although weather conditions had not improved, we made preparations for another lengthy bus journey. Our intention was to visit Rabat – a suburb of Mdina, in order to have access to the Catacombs dedicated to Saint Paul and

---

[6] *'The 32,00 tons of supplies enabled Malta to stave off the target date for the island's surrender which was the week of September in 1942'.*

Saint Agatha. While Rabat is situated over a honeycomb of tunnels and caverns, some of which are catacombs dating from late Roman and Byzantine times, others are natural caves used for even earlier burials; in more recent times they provided shelters during World War 11.

The earliest archaeological evidence of Christianity in Malta is to be found in these catacombs. In Roman times they were used to lay the dead to rest – the Romans believed it was unhygienic to bury the dead in the city. Early Christians later used the catacombs to secretly practice their religious beliefs. Saint Paul's catacombs are just one of the possible places on the island where tradition states that he lived and preached Christianity.

Other, previously visited sites include the former estate of the Roman Governor, Publius which lies a couple of miles south of Saint Paul's Island, now marked by the small seventeenth-century of 'Church of *San Pawl Milqi'* (Saint Paul Welcomed); the Apostle's Fountain, near the head of Saint Paul's Bay; the Church of Saint Paul's Bonfire, Bugibba; Saint Paul's Cathedral in Mdina, built over a small fourth-century church on the supposed site where the Publius, the Roman Governor of Malta was converted to Christianity.

The bus route took us up and down hills and through narrow streets. As we drew nearer to Rabat, we had lovely views of the Knights' former stronghold of Mdina, crowning the hillside. When we arrived at the bus terminus in Rabat, we followed signs directing us to Saint Paul's Square, where the 'Church of Saint Paul Outside the Walls' is, quite literally positioned outside Mdina's fortified walls. The church has been built over a series of caves and tunnels that link to the nearby Grotto of Saint Paul as well as to Saint Agatha's Catacombs. According to tradition the Grotto is the place where, after he was shipwrecked Paul took refuge and stayed for three months trying to convert local people to Christianity. It was during this time that he was invited to the house of Publius, the Roman's chief man on the island and cured the father of Publius of a serious fever. Publius is then said to have then been converted to Christianity and was made the first Bishop of Malta.

At the entrance to the nearby museum, we were able to purchase tickets for entry to both Saint Paul's Grotto and Saint Agatha's Catacombs. The entrance to Saint Paul's led to two large rock-hewn areas: the crypt containing the remains of a rock-hewn altar used for church services and a rock-hewn agate table where mourners gathered to hold a 'wake': farewell meal in memory of the deceased. From the crypt a tunnel led to a labyrinth of narrow rock-cut stairways and corridors lit by the occasional overhead light, between tombs for both children and adults. We learnt that the corpse was embalmed with oil and spices and balsam, covered with a long shroud and wrapped with bandages. The body was then laid in the grave and later covered with stone slabs and sealed with mortar. It was an atmospheric and sobering experience that emphasised the courageousness of Saint Paul and those early Christians who faced persecution for practicing their religious belief. It was a relief to escape into the sunlit square before making our way to the entrance to Saint Agatha's Catacombs.

Although Saint Agatha lived in Mdina, she is said to have sought refuge in the catacombs to pray to escape persecution of the Emperor Decius (249–251) AD for refusing to marry Quintianus, the Governor of Sicily, who had fallen in love with her. The Maltese kept the catacombs in her memory. Our priority was to visit the crypt in order to see the frescoes painted over the walls and altar, dedicated to the memory of her. We made our way along a narrow walkway between houses until we came upon an alabaster statue of the saint. Situated at the entrance to a tree-lined, paved walkway, it led to the entrance to the museum.

Unfortunately, we arrived to find that as a result of the passage of time, as well as adverse climate conditions the frescoes had fallen into a state of disrepair and were currently undergoing restoration, so we were unable to see the original artwork. However, we were able to see copies that were on display in the museum. Altogether there were 13 depictions of St Agatha, as well as of those saints associated with her including a trio of frescoes that featured St Lucy, St Venera and St Agatha, representing virgin martyrdom. There was also an image of St Leonard, the patron saint of slaves, holding chains in solidarity with captives – possibly giving relevance to the ongoing persecution of Christians by the Ottomans at that time. A fresco dating from the 4th century shows the Alpha and Omega – signifying Christ as God – the beginning and the end of life; a large scallop shell represented heaven; two doves represented the souls of the departed while the scattering of flowers portrayed eternal life.

Once again, the terrible suffering that Christians underwent was verified by the visit to the catacombs – this time by the remarkable frescoes, albeit copies in the museum. As we made our way back to Saint Paul's Square our intention was to visit the church. Unfortunately, we arrived to see a funeral gathering outside. A nearby café came to our rescue for a recovery snack before the bus journey back to Sliema and our final night at the lovely 'Preluna Hotel and Spa' on the historic island of Malta.

Paul completes his journey from Malta to Rome

After spending three months on Malta, as spring approached Paul knew that the time for him to continue his journey to Rome was near. An Alexandrian ship, wintering on Malta with passengers and grain cargo, heading for Rome was waiting for the start of the sailing season. When the day came for the ship to leave Paul, accompanied by Luke is put on board. They set sail through the narrow Messina Straits between Sicily and the tip of Italy to Rhegium. On the following day they sail against strong winds to Puteoli, in the Bay of Naples. Since the ship was too large to dock in Rome's harbour, the grain had to be transferred to a smaller vessel. This would take a good deal of time so Paul, together with Luke is granted a seven day stop over at Puteoli before completing the journey to Rome on foot. During this time, they were relieved to discover a small group of Christian believers with whom they had the opportunity to spend time. Then on the approach to Rome, Paul and Luke received further encouragement when they are met and greeted by 'brothers', who had received news of their arrival. 'When Paul saw them, he thanked God and took courage'. (Acts 28:15)

On his arrival in Rome Paul is allowed to stay in his own accommodation, under the guard of a soldier for a period of two years. During this time, he is visited by a large number of people and is able to put his case before them, as well as telling them about the Kingdom of God and the truth about Jesus Christ the Saviour of the world. Although Paul lives in the hope that he will be set free he is ready and willing to face martyrdom if that is the outcome. Finally, in AD (68) he is brought to stand trial before Nero. Condemned to death he is led out of the city-gates and beheaded. As a Roman citizen he was spared the indignity of crucifixion suffered by Peter, after he stood trial in the Circus of Nero in Rome. Not only does Peter suffer crucifixion but believing that he is not worthy to be put to death in the same way as Christ he requested the further indignity and suffering of being crucified upside down.

*****

An invitation to partake in a pilgrimage to Rome and Assisi with Father Mark and fellow parishioners from Saint Mary's Parish was an opportunity to visit the magnificent basilicas dedicated to both Saint Peter and Saint Paul, as well as the Vatican – the home of Pope Francis. From Rome the pilgrimage continues through the Umbrian Mountains to Assisi – the homeland of Saint Francis, the saint who the present pope chooses to be named after – a fitting place to bring an unforgettable journey to an end.

Rome and Assisi Pilgrimage

Rome

Our journey began with an early morning flight from Gatwick to Rome's Fiumicino Airport. Met by a guide we were then transported by coach for lunch at a local restaurant in preparation for our first tour: a visit to the 'Basilica of St Paul Outside the Walls'. Erected under the instructions of the Emperor Constantine in A.D. 324, over the burial place of Saint Paul, the basilica was built to commemorate the execution and martyrdom of the apostle – its name applies to its position 'outside' the original Aurelian Walls that once surrounded Rome.

The approach through an imposing courtyard, lined with 150 columns, led to the feet of a towering marble statue of Saint Paul; holding the sword of his execution he is positioned in the centre of the courtyard with his back to the entrance of the basilica. The magnificence of the building before us outshone its complex past including a disastrous fire in 1823. We paused to take in the details of a remarkable gold mosaics on the façade, over the statue's head. At the apex Christ is portrayed between the Apostles Peter and Paul. Between this and a lower section, showing Old Testament prophets is an image of the Lamb of God on the Mountain of Paradise, surrounded by four rivers symbolising the four Gospels and twelve lambs representing the twelve Apostles.

As we follow the guide through the central bronze door, the sense of the basilica's magnitude and splendour is further enhanced by four rows of columns supporting arcaded entablatures, decorated with circular portraitures of 267 popes. Amidst these and so much treasured artwork and history commemorating the life and death of Saint Paul, I was especially moved by a visit to the chapel where Saint Ignatius and his followers – founders of the Jesuits – took their vows. A final image that stays with me is that of a Venetian mosaic over the apse depicting the enthroned figure of Christ accompanied by Peter, Paul, Andreas and Luke.

From the burial place of Saint Paul to the underground heart of Rome: in the fifth century BC a law forbidding Romans to bury their dead within the city was passed. The *Via Appia* – an ancient Roman road leading out of the city– was decided upon as a place for burying the dead underground. Carved out of soft volcanic rock, there are said to be at least 200 miles of tombs. We were heading for the San Callisto Catacombs known as a place where Christians, threatened with persecution, practised their faith and buried their dead.

Met at the entrance by an on-site guide we were taken to stand before a display of copies of some of the original frescoes, carvings and drawings depicting ancient Christian symbols; the guide explained that, over the years invasions of Rome resulted in a large number of the frescoes being destroyed or taken. Images of remaining and recovered frescoes include scenes from the last supper, Christ holding the gospel, shepherds with their flocks, anchors as symbols of the cross and doves as symbols of peace. The most moving image is that of Saint Cecelia, the patroness of music: of a noble family she was martyred in the third century and entombed where her statue now lies.

We followed the guide into and through one of the deep tunnels that lead through four levels of extensive underground galleries – the walls on either side lined with niches and vaults where the enshrouded bodies of the dead were left. From time to time an archway, carved into the rock face, marked the entrance to the vault of a wealthy family. Our tour ended at a small enclave at the end of a tunnel that had been especially set up as a place to celebrate mass; without seating and without decoration, the absolute simplicity of nothing except an altar and missal stand was a reminder of the threats faced by the early Christians. This was the place where we shared mass with Father Mark: a moving end to our first day in Rome.

As the day drew to a close weary travellers arrived at the guesthouse, run by the Bridgettine Sisters: a splendid upmarket location alongside the French Embassy and overlooking Farnese Square. In 1847 French embassy staff moved into the former late Renaissance Palace: Palazzo Farnese at the heart of medieval Rome; twin fountains, standing at the centre of the square – each marked with a stone sculpted iris – remain as symbols of the royal Farnese family. Met and escorted by one of the sisters we were handed keys and given directions to our simply but adequately furnished rooms. Further explorations revealed that while the sisters had a secluded inner courtyard to retire to, we had the pleasure of sharing their chapel as well as the use of a splendid roof terrace garden. A further advantage was that the guesthouse was within walking distance of the River Tiber and the Vatican.

*****

After breakfast, on the following morning we headed for the largest church in Rome dedicated to the Blessed Virgin Mary: *Basilica di Sancta Maria Maggiore*. Tradition has it that the Virgin Mary inspired the choice of the Esquiline Hill for the location of the church. Appearing in a dream to both Patrician John and Pope Liberius (352–366), she asked that the church be built in her honour on the top of the hill. The following morning, the hill was covered by an unexpected fall of snow. Nevertheless, the pope traced the perimeter of the proposed basilica in the snow while John financed the construction. 'Our Lady of the Snows' as the basilica became known, was so named in the Roman missal from 1568–1969. To this day white petals are scattered from the dome of the chapel to celebrate the anniversary of the fall of snow.

As we entered the building the sense of being immersed in centuries of talented architectural styles of columns, arches, mosaics and frescoes was once again almost overpowering. This, plus 16th and 17th century chapels dedicated to various popes, with artwork associated with prominent artists including frescoes by Reni and Della Porta all added to a determination to keep alive memories of a complex religious past. Among the plethora of images, the most potent include – a statue of Pope Pius ix kneeling before wooden pieces of the manger in the crypt, under the high altar and a rose-stained glass window. Created in 1995 for the main façade by Giovanni Hajnal, the design centres on the figure of Mary cradling the infant Jesus in her lap; to symbolise the Old Testament Hajnal included an image of the seven branched candlestick; for the New Testament he used the chalice of the Eucharist.

Lunch followed by a coach ride helped clear our heads and prepared us for a dramatic change of scene: a visit to the Colosseum. In the company of Richard, our historian guide, we were transported into the Gladiatorial Era of Ancient Rome. This time there were no reminders of saintly figures but plenty of gladiators, prisoners, lions and wild animals, as well as emperors and bloodthirsty crowds. As we entered through an archway into the amphitheatre and made our way to a row of seats Richard reminded us that the Colosseum was once capable of holding 55,000 spectators in its four-story tiered seating – with 80 entrance arcades and special seating in the lower sections for the emperor, senators and vestal virgins. Now in full flow, he was explaining that the amphitheatre was in active use over some four centuries until the struggles of the Western Roman Empire and a gradual change in public tastes put an end to gladiatorial combats and other large public entertainments. By the sixth century AD, the arena had suffered severe damage due to natural phenomena such as lightning and earthquakes.

In the centuries to come, the Colosseum was abandoned completely, and used as a quarry for numerous building projects, including the cathedrals of Saint Peter and Saint John Lateran as well as for defence fortifications along the Tiber River. Beginning in the 18th century various popes sought to conserve the arena as a sacred Christian site. Then in the 1990s restoration work began and has proceeded over the years. That work was still in progress was evident all round us, especially on the floor of the arena. The size and magnificence of the remaining sections was a powerful reminder of both the splendour and horrors of Imperial Rome.

It was on our return to the accommodation that we discovered the downside to its otherwise upmarket position. It was Saturday evening – the time when Italians fill the restaurants and bars that spill into the square and along neighbouring cobbled streets. Just as we were preparing to leave for a night's rest after an enjoyable evening spent on the rooftop terrace, neighbourhood Italians were gathering to celebrate the end of the week. This varied from an increasing volume of chatting and singing to shouting, punctuated, at times with fighting. Windows closed and fingers in ears had little or no effect on the volume, which fluctuated in intensity and nature until daybreak.

The following morning, breakfast, served by the sisters, was an aid to partial recovery in preparation for the second highlight of our itinerary in Rome: a visit to St Peter's Basilica.

*****

Described as 'standing like a sentinel guarding the Vatican City' the dome of the basilica continues to bear witness to its past and present. Once again on my travels I was reminded of the powerful influence of the Emperor Constantine who, in A.D. 324, commissioned the church to be built over the tomb of Saint Peter: a larger, grander version of 'St Paul Outside the Walls'. The square, the fountain, columns and statues, as well a plethora of the work of great Renaissance and Baroque artists – the basilica not only overshadows other basilicas in Rome but throughout the world.

Our focus was to celebrate Latin said Sunday mass in the basilica. Before the service started, we had time to take in some of the splendour before us. The most compelling memories include standing before Michelangelo's marble sculpture *The Pieta*: a moving and beautiful rendition of a youthful Virgin Mary cradling the dead body of her son. More than any other art forms the talent of sculpture fills me with awe: carved from a single piece of marble in 1499, *The Pieta* remains high on my list of most admired masterpieces. Returning to the nave my eyes were drawn towards Bernini's massive bronze canopy over the Papal Altar – built over the tomb of Saint Peter. Looking up, running round the interior of the dome – a Latin inscription in letters more than six' high – are the unforgettable words of Christ: *"You are Peter, and on this rock, I will build my church...And I will give you the keys of the kingdom of heaven."* (Matthew 16 18–19)

The Latin mass was to be said in a large chapel near the front of the basilica. We arrived to find the area cordoned off – we could attend but not fully participate. A number of cardinals wearing red robes, bishops wearing white robes and mitres as well as musicians and a choir contributed to the service while those visitors, who had pre-booked were seated in rows before the altar. The choral rendition of the mass brought back memories of my father's love of the Latin mass, so much so that on a regular basis he would travel from our Surrey home to attend the service at Westminster Cathedral.

When we finally made our way out of the basilica it was to find the steps and the entire square filled with people. It was approaching noon and Pope Francis was expected to appear from a top right-hand window of the Vatican Palace, alongside the basilica, to say the Angelus. The window was sheltered by a small canopy and marked by the red papal flag. Our timing was perfect but our position on the crowded steps less so. The steps and the square below were filled with people who had gathered in readiness for the Pope's appearance. As we struggled to find a space with a view to the window the Angelus bells rang out and the pope's arm raised in greeting to the cheering crowd – appeared. Sadly, such was my position that was my restricted view. Then his magnified voice led us through the Angelus; as it ended his arm was raised in a farewell blessing and the crowd cheered once more. My dream of an encounter with Pope Francis – no matter how distant and limited – had been achieved.

*****

On our final day we had the choice of various guided tours including that of the Sistine Chapel. This was not my first trip to Rome. A previous visit had included this outstanding chapel.

I had reached the stage of feeling overwhelmed by architecture and artwork, no matter how magnificent. I needed space. Camera and street plan in hand I set off across the square, down a narrow, cobbled street, under and alongside archways and roadside fountains until I reached the River Tiber. Right before me was Ponte Sisto Bridge. Commissioned by Pope Sixtus IV, after whom it is named, it was built on the remains of the former Pons Aurelius Bridge and has extensive views both up and down the Tiber. As I made my way to the centre of the bridge and looked upriver, the cupola of Saint Peter's was there before me. Then as I turned to look downriver a swallow dipped over my head; for one unforgettable moment I was transported into the mystical ambience of both the natural and spiritual worlds surrounding me.

A set of steps took me to the side of the river where I continued downstream; a lone traveller with nothing but the shushing of water and the occasional fisherman to accompany me, I made my way past two more bridges towards the outline of a monastery on the far side, identifiable by the carved silhouette of a saintly figure against the sky.

On my return I stopped for a croissant and coffee at one of a number of bars and restaurants that spill into the square, where a local violinist serenaded me. I arrived at the guesthouse just in time to join fellow pilgrims for the next stage of our journey to the fortified, settlement of Assisi. That the present pope chose to be named after Saint Francis, who had dedicated his life to helping those in need, made our visit to the place where the saint lived, worked and died, appropriate and special.

Assisi

A coach ride through the Umbrian Mountains and across wide, open plains then uphill again took us to the medieval city. Set on the side of Monte Subasio, it is the place where Francis was born in 1182 and where he made the life-changing decision to renounce his wealthy lifestyle and possessions so that he could help the sick and those in need. It was also the place where a young woman, named Clare heard Francis preaching and became one of his followers. Our sights were set upon those churches and places that are memorials to both saints.

Finally, the coach detoured onto a winding road that took us to another guesthouse run by the Bridgettine sisters. Its lovely rural, hillside setting, fronted by extensive terraced gardens, also came with views down and across the Umbrian hillside, marked with the outlines of basilicas, as well as up to Assisi.

Our introduction to the city was to meet with a local guide at *Porta Nuova* – the first of a number of medieval arches that mark the route along the main cobbled street, leading to churches and historic sites. After receiving a brief history of Assisi as well as of the lives of both saints we were escorted to *Piazza Chiesa Nuova* to stand before statues of Saint Francis' parents. Discarded clothes held by his father and broken chains, by his mother, symbolise his renouncement of a wealthy lifestyle and his freedom. We continued past the Roman façade and Corinthian columns marking the entrance of the former Temple of Minerva – now the church of *Santa Maria Sopra Minerva* and on to the Basilica of Saint Francis; this, the final resting place of the saint, is reputed to be the second most important basilica in Italy. While the size and comparatively simple outline of the building bear no comparison to St Peter's – its associations with the saint as well as the number and variety of magnificent frescoes, highlighting definitive moments in his spiritual life, attract visitors and pilgrims world-wide.

As we made our way along the nave towards steps leading to the burial place of the saint, I was distracted by a side chapel, dedicated to Saint Martin of Tours. Like Saint Francis the saint came from a wealthy family and had dreams of military glory; then, a mounted Roman officer on horseback, he had an unexpected encounter with a roadside beggar, which led him to cut his cloak in half and to give half to the beggar. It is said that the following night he had a dream of Christ wearing the part of the cloak he had given away. There before me were two wall panels with frescoes portraying the incident and the dream.

The surprising thing about the saint and the frescoes was that just weeks previously I had visited the ancient Anglo-Saxon town of Wareham in my home county of Dorset. My primary interest had been to stand before the effigy of Lawrence of Arabia in the oldest surviving 11th century Saxon church in Wareham – that of Saint Martin. In addition to the remarkable effigy, I chanced upon some faded frescoes on the north wall of the chancel – one depicting Saint Martin on horseback, dividing his cloak to give half to a naked beggar – a replica of the fresco before me.

I was distracted from my musings by the sudden appearance of Father Mark. "Quick," he called. "Come quickly. I've been given permission to say mass." I followed him to catch up with fellow pilgrims, down a stairway to a small chapel beneath the basilica. It was a rather sombre place but certainly unique, especially the altar and missal stand; supported by sawn off sections of the branching trunk of a tree it was a true reminder of the saint's determination to live a simple life devoted to prayer: a special and memorable place to share mass with Father Mark.

From the final resting place of Francis to that of Saint Clare: The *Basilica di Santa Chiara*. Our focus: to visit The Chapel of the Crucifix – so named because tradition states that the 12th century wooden crucifix in the chapel is believed to be the original one from which Francis heard Christ asking him to 'repair' his church while at prayer in the chapel of San Damiano. Standing before the crucifix brought back a sense of the miraculous moment that heralded a deep spiritual purpose in the saint's life. Finally, a set of dark stairs took us down to the crypt where Saint Clare was laid to rest.

This sombre end to our introduction to Assisi was very soon to be lightened. The coach took us on a fifteen-minute, zigzag downhill route to the guesthouse. We arrived in time to enjoy sundowners on the terrace enhanced by views across the Umbrian countryside, the soft tolling of church bells and the rose-coloured sky, flecked and threaded by the outlines of swooping swallows.

The following morning, we set off heading for the neighbouring hilltop city of Perugia. A mighty Etruscan centre and medieval city, Perugia has become a major tourist and cultural destination. A twenty-minute coach ride across Umbrian plains, through fields of vineyards and olive groves then into the mountains: over bridges and through a narrow tunnel to a winding avenue of beech trees that ended at the foot of the medieval walls surrounding the city. Access by stone stairways and/or escalators led to *Piazza Italia* – an Italian

Square: grassy areas dotted with benches and decorated with statues of eminent historic figures, shaded by huge fir trees – it was a lovely and convenient meeting place.

We were greeted by Anna, a local guide, who enlightened us with a brief history of Perugia before leading us along the main cobbled high street, lined with ancient churches and buildings to *Fontana Maggiore*: a monumental two-tier medieval fountain located between the Cathedral of *San Lorenzo* and *Palazzo dei Priori* (medieval town hall).

We learned that in the 13th century Perugia relied on water taken from ancient wells, then between 1254 and 1276 an aqueduct was built to provide fresh water; in 1275 its completion was celebrated by erecting the fountain. As we made our way a sense of a much fought over past was evident in both the architecture and sculptured figures – those of lions and griffins were especially prominent on the frontage of buildings. While the lion is a symbol of the Guelph party who supported the papacy, the griffin symbolises 13th century Perugia's reliance on water taken from ancient wells.

Minutes later we were standing before the fountain taking in its size and the range of sculptures; made up of two concentric polygonal basins, the lower one featuring bas-reliefs of the twelve months of the year, accompanied by signs of the zodiac while the upper one is decorated with twenty-four small statues representing symbols, saints and historical characters. Its history is just as fascinating. Built between 1277 and 1278, to celebrate the completion of an aqueduct that carried water from *Monte Pacciano* directly into the square, it remains a main tourist attraction to this day.

Anna was directing us to follow her towards San Lorenzo Cathedral, one side of which 'gives' onto the square. The cathedral's reputation as the main religious edifice of Perugia is believed to be centred on a legend that it is the depository of the Virgin Mary's wedding ring, said to have been stolen in 1473 from the nearby town of Chiusi.

We followed Anna along a side aisle to the chapel where the ring is kept under lock and key in a gilded container. She explained that the ring is displayed on two days every year: July 30th – to commemorate the day it was brought to Perugia and on the last Saturday in January – Mary's wedding anniversary. Anna then admitted that although the legend has long since been disproved it continues to attract visitors to Perugia and so is good for the local economy. As we prepared to return to the square Anna bade us farewell – we were free to have lunch at one of a number of enticing cafes or restaurants and for further explorations of the fascinating medieval city before meeting at the Italian Square, in readiness for a return lift to the guesthouse.

*****

Our final day began with a visit to San Damiano, the little church where it all began for Saint Francis and was also central to the life of Saint Clare. The route wound down hill into the rural setting of Umbria. Met and guided by Father John, a Franciscan monk, we were taken into the Crucifix Chapel: the place where Christ is said to have spoken to Francis from the cross. We followed Father John through a doorway to the right of the altar and into the choir of the Poor Clares; it was here that in 1212 Francis brought Clare to the place where she and the sisters who joined her, spent their frugal lives. This was wholly evident in the sparsely furnished rooms – especially the dormitory where the sisters slept on straw mats.

A narrow staircase led to Clare's Garden, especially notable for a statue of Saint Francis seated cross legged on the grass in an attitude of contemplation; nearby stands a stone block on which is engraved, in Umbrian dialect, the following line from The Canticle of the Creatures: '*Praise be to You my Lord with all Your Creatures*'. Both images are reminders of the saint's love of the natural world and that it was here that he wrote this section of the canticle.

Towards the end of his life, at a time when he was suffering immense physical pain from the stigmata wounds that he had received two years previously, he was brought to San Damiano to be looked after by Saint Clare. A few days before his death – at his request – he was laid naked upon the earth where it is said that he sang the Canticle's Praises of God.

Lunch at a hotel's upmarket restaurant with fellow pilgrims brought a complete change of scene and mood. The only person, sharing the restaurant with us was a priest who was pre-occupied writing in his notebook while waiting for his lunch to be served. Then an Italian waiter turned his attention to our table. From the start he was charming and mildly flirtatious to the female members of the group. As the meal progressed – much to our amusement – his flirtations became more pronounced, culminating in an on one knee, marriage proposal to Elizabeth, a fellow pilgrim – mainly for the benefit of our flashing cameras. My concern that we were disturbing the priest was unfounded. He was smiling widely and obviously enjoying the hilarity of this unexpected scenario.

Some mind adjustment was needed before our final visit. This time to the basilica of *Santa Maria degli Angeli* – celebrated as the home of the *Porziuncola*: a small chapel that became the nucleus of the first Franciscan monastery. In addition, the chapel commemorates the Assisi Pardon: the indulgences received from Pope Honorius for the forgiveness of confessed and repented sins. The Feast of the Pardon, attended by pilgrims from all over the world, takes place in August each year. The basilica was also the place where Saint Francis established the Order of the Poor Clares.

Once again it was the range of frecoes depicting extraordinary times in the saints' lives that brought these moments to life – notably one of Clare when, supported by a candle bearing monk, she is shown wearing the newly received habit given to her by Saint Francis. An image of Francis receiving the stigmata wounds is especially moving and confirmation of his desire to not only to follow in the footsteps of Christ but to share his suffering.

Mass in small side chapel, the altar supported by a stone replica of the branching tree in San Damiano, confirming the close spiritual empathy between Francis and Clare brought our visit to a close. The moving prayer attributed to Saint Francis brings the account of my journey to a close.

Prayer of Saint Francis

Lord, make me an instrument of Your peace.
Where there is hatred, let me bring love.
Where there is injury, let me bring pardon.
Where there is discord, let me bring union.
Where there is doubt, let me bring faith.
Where there is error, let me bring truth,
Where there is despair let me bring hope,
Where there is sadness, let me bring joy,
Where there is darkness, let me bring light.
Divine Master, grant that I may not so much
Seek to be consoled as to console,
To be understood as to understand,

To be loved as to love.
It is in pardoning that we are pardoned.
It is in dying that we are born to eternal life.

Selective Bibliography

The Holy Land, The Land of Jesus, (Palphot, July 2004)

The Collins Atlas of Bible History, Edited: James Pritchard & Nick Page (Harper Collins, 2008)

The New Jerusalem Bible, New Testament Readers' Edition (Darton, Longman & Todd Ltd, 1991)

Encyclopaedia Britannica / Catholic Encyclopaedia

Colin Thubron, *Journey into Cyprus* (Penguin Books, 1986)

George Mc Donald, *Cyprus Spiral Guide* (AA Publishing 2006)

Paul Harcourt Davis, Cyprus Globetrotter (New Holland, 2002)

Lawrence Durrell, *Bitter Lemons of Cyprus* (Faber, 1957)

Vassos Karageorghis, Ecclesiastical Treasury, *Chrysorrogiatissa Monastery* (G. Leventis Anastasios, 2003)

A. Papgeorgio, *The Monastery of Agios Neophytos* (Nicosia, 2005)

Giorgos Kakkouras, *Saint Nicolas of The Roof* (Trans. Dr Andreas Vitti, 2005)

Peter Walker, *In the Steps of Saint Paul* (Lion Hudson, 2011)

Richard Stoneman, *A Traveller's History of Turkey* (The Armchair Traveller at the book Haus, 2011)

William Dalrymple, *From the Holy Mountain* (Harper Perennial, 1997)

William Dalrymple, *In Xanadu* (Harper Collins, 1990)

M.Salahattin Erdemgil, *Ephesus* (Duru Basim YaynYaym Reklamcilik ve Gida San Tic Ltd. Sti.)

Paul Harcourt Davis, *Rhodes, Globetrotter Travel Guide* (New Holland, 2015)

Lawrence Durrell, *Reflections on a Marine Venus* (Faber & Faber, 2015)

Paul Hellander & Jeanne Oliver, *Crete* (Lonely Planet, 2002)

Juliet Rix, *Malta and Gozo* (Bradt Travel Guide, Edition 3)

Pat Levy & Sean Shehan, *Malta & Gozo, Essential Spiral* (AA Publishing 2007)

Raymond Goodburn, *A Pilgrim's Guide to Rome & Assisi* (Pilgrim Book Services 2010) www.biblicalarchaeology.org